WHY
believe?

WHY
believe?

Roger Carswell

OM PUBLISHING
Carlisle, U.K.

British Library Cataloguing in Publication Data
Carswell, Roger
Why Believe?
1. Christian doctrine
I. Title
230

ISBN 1 85078 079 X

OM Publishing is an imprint of STL Ltd.,
PO Box 300, Carlisle, Cumbria, CA3 0QS, U.K.

Production and Printing in the U.K. by
Nuprint Ltd, Station Road, Harpenden, Herts, AL5 4SE.

Dedication

Dedicated to Dot.
She is not only my best friend but also my best
critic, counsellor and companion. I respect her as
a Christian and love her as my wife.

Acknowledgements

I want to take this opportunity to express my appreciation to Mrs Christine Watts of Leeds. She has laboured hard and long in preparing the manuscript, showing great patience throughout. Her life and work is a demonstration of the vigour God gives to those who believe.

Contents

Introduction

The Bible does not seek to prove God's existence; it treats it as fact. The Bible's opening words are: 'In the beginning God...'[1]

By contrast, however, from schoolchildren to senior citizens, the argument as to whether or not God exists continues. Words are without number when it comes to quoting from the seemingly endless debate. The Bible teaches that there is a basic dishonesty in the heart of every atheist. 'The fool has said in his heart, "There is no God," '[2] or, as the thrust of the meaning of the verse implies, the fool has said in his heart, 'No God for me.' In other words, it is not so much that people cannot believe but that they will not. In the New Testament we read that:

> His invisible attributes are clearly seen...even his eternal power and Godhead, so that [people] are without excuse, because, although they knew God, they did not glorify him as God, nor were thankful, but became futile in their thoughts, and their foolish hearts were darkened. Professing to be wise, they became fools, and changed the glory of the incorruptible God into an image made like corruptible man—and birds and four-footed beasts and creeping things. Therefore God also gave them up to uncleanness...[3]

God has revealed himself to mankind.

Of course, we will never, as finite beings, be able to

9

understand fully all the qualities and attributes of the infinite God. God is too great for small man to comprehend and he is too holy for sinful man to reach. However, God has revealed himself and reached down to rescue us.

I have written elsewhere[4] that God has revealed himself to mankind in five basic ways. First, through creation—the material word; second, through individual conscience—the unspoken word; third, through Scripture—the written word; fourth, through Christ—the living and loving Word; and fifth, through Christian conversion—the experienced word.

In this book we will explore some of these aspects of God's revelation to his world. We will merely scrape the surface of evidence, which in totality is vast. The apostle John wrote at the end of his Gospel, 'And there are also many other things that Jesus did, which if they were written one by one, I suppose that even the world itself could not contain the books that would be written.'[5] However, the Bible speaks of 'many infallible proofs'[6] concerning Christ and his resurrection. The evidence of the truth of the gospel is overwhelming, and may be experienced by those who will, with an open mind, seek God.

On 25 August 1965 I was converted to Christ. I shall never forget that day. As a teenager I was on holiday in the Lebanon, staying with relatives who were involved in Christian medical work in Beirut and beyond. Their consistent character and caring lives made a deep impression upon me. I began to ask myself questions such as, 'What is a Christian?' and 'Why are these people so different from me?' or 'Why do they live for others and I for myself?'

I had been brought up in a home where my parents had taught me about God and the Lord Jesus and had set a fine example of Christian behaviour. However, as a young person I had drifted away from the things of God.

My life and language betrayed a restlessness and rebellion within. But I knew that there was more to life than living for the moment.

After a game of tennis, an uncle, the Reverend Hagop Sagharian, began to chat through the gospel message. Using a pocket New Testament he explained step by step my position before God and God's method of restoring me to being the person he intended me to be.

He turned me to Romans chapter 3 verse 23 and asked me to read aloud the words: 'For all have sinned and fall short of the glory of God.' I was well aware of wrong within. My attitude to God, my parents and others was far from what I knew to be right. God's holiness and my sinfulness felt a reality to me.

We turned to Romans chapter 6 verse 23 and again I read aloud: 'For the wages of sin is death, but the gift of God is eternal life in Christ Jesus our Lord.' My uncle explained how sin not only separated me from God now but ultimately would send me to hell. Then he explained the cross. God's great rescue mission was bound up in Jesus Christ coming to earth. God himself had come to earth in the person of Christ. Again, we looked in Romans. This time it was chapter 5 verse 8: 'But God demonstrates his own love toward us, in that while we were still sinners, Christ died for us.'

Graphically, it was explained that the Lord had laid on Jesus my sin. He was the substitute dying in my place, paying for my sin. I had never understood that before. I felt that if God loved me enough for Christ to die for me, then the least I could do was trust him.

Christ not only died but rose again. Things began to fall into place in my mind. Jesus had died to offer me forgiveness and three days later had risen. He was therefore able to give power over sin and death. God, by his Holy Spirit, could come and live in my life.

Simply, sitting on a log in the mountains of Lebanon, overlooking Beirut, I prayed and trusted Christ as my

Lord and Saviour. I thanked him for dying for me and asked him to forgive me and make me his for ever. There was no flash in the sky, but neither was this a flash in the pan.

God became real to me and totally changed my aims, ambitions and affections. This was the beginning of a personal relationship with him, which has grown deeper as the years have passed on. It was also the start of finding out about both who God is and what he has done.

We read in the Bible that there is only one God.[7] God, however, has multiple personality. As a human being is only one, yet is body, soul and spirit,[8] so God who made man in his own image is Father, Son and Holy Spirit.[9] That is why, for example, God said, 'Let us make man in our image.'[10]

Christians describe God as 'the Trinity': one God who is in three persons and three persons who are one. Significantly the Bible, which speaks of the Father, Son and Holy Spirit, ascribes to each attributes that are only God's. From the Bible we also discover many other attributes of his. We learn that he is:

Spirit (John 4:24)
Personal (John 17:1–3)
Omnipotent, or all-powerful (Revelation 19:6)
Omnipresent (Psalm 139:7–12)
Omniscient, or all-knowing (1 John 3:20)
Wise (Acts 15:18)
Infinite (1 Kings 8:27)
Eternal (Isaiah 57:15)
Invisible (John 1:18)
Unchangeable (Numbers 23:19)
Unequalled (Isaiah 40:13–25)
Holy (Revelation 4:8)
Just (Psalm 89:14)
Patient (Exodus 34:6,7)
Merciful (Lamentations 3:22,23)

Wrathful (Deuteronomy 32:22)
Loving (1 John 4:8,16)
Everlasting (Habakkuk 3:6)
True (Revelation 15:3)
etc., etc....

Perhaps these at present seem distant to you. They are just a list. All mankind wants to find out why we exist. The three great questions we ask are, 'Where have I come from?', 'What am I doing?' and 'Where am I going?' Modern-day fascination with the supernatural not only reveals a despair about the state of the present world but an awareness of another dimension to our existence.

God does not want us to flounder in the dark. He, our maker, has devised means whereby we who ought to be banished from him can be brought into a relationship with him. The gospel was summarised by the apostle Paul when he wrote: 'For I delivered to you first of all that which I also received: that Christ died for our sins according to the Scriptures, and that he was buried, and that he rose again the third day according to the Scriptures.'[11]

Is this the greatest hoax ever to inflict itself on the history of the world? Or, is it in reality God's truth? I trust that reading the chapters of this book will help answer the vital question, 'Why believe?'

Notes

1. Genesis 1:1.
2. Psalm 14:1.
3. Romans 1:20–24.
4. Roger Carswell, *How Small a Whisper* (Baker Book House, 1989).
5. John 21:25.
6. Acts 1:3.

7. Deuteronomy 6:4.
8. 1 Thessalonians 5:23.
9. See Isaiah 6:3; John 14:26; 15:26; Matthew 28:18,19; 1 John 5:7; 2 Corinthians 13:14; as well as the many verses that prove that both the Holy Spirit and Jesus are themselves God.
10. Genesis 1:26.
11. 1 Corinthians 15:3,4.

1

Why Believe the Bible Is the Word of God?

Jesus said: *The words that I speak to you are spirit, and they are life.*
John 6:63

For nearly two thousand years the Bible has been attacked, insulted, mocked or ignored. Although the world's best seller, in some quarters it is in danger of becoming just another 'classic'—a book everybody has heard of but nobody has read. In many countries today it is a forbidden book; while on the one hand attempting to discredit it, even governments sense its power. In some ways a chapter seeking to prove the Bible to be the word of God would be rendered unnecessary if only people would read the Scriptures for themselves. God's word carries its own authenticity and authority.

Consider, for example, the story of a husband, wife and daughter who went to a series of gospel meetings in a village church near Wakefield in March 1984. They were not Christians, but they were considering spiritual issues. At the Wednesday children's meeting the girl was given a memory verse: 'The wages of sin is death, but the gift of God is eternal life through Jesus Christ our Lord' (Romans 6:23). The mother helped the daughter to learn the verse. As a family they attended each meeting, but gave their apologies for their absence on the Saturday because they were attending a wedding.

After the wedding and reception, some guests went to a local public house for the evening. A comedian was booked to entertain them. One sketch involved him dressing up as a monk and carrying a banner on which were the words, 'The wages of sin is death.' His derisive mockery was misplaced. God's word struck to the heart of the woman, who left the pub, went home and trusted Jesus Christ. Her husband received Christ as Saviour and Lord the very next day. The truth of God's word had broken into their world and turned their lives around.

God is not isolated from his creation, abrogating responsibility for it. He has not left man in the lurch. Apart from creation itself, he has revealed himself to mankind in two fundamental ways—through the loving and living Word, Jesus Christ, who himself fulfils the word; and through the written word, the Bible, which itself reveals Christ. There follow five reasons why I believe the Bible is the word of God.

1. It is human, yet divine

The Bible was written over a period of sixteen hundred years by about forty authors. Some were sovereigns, others subjects; some were lawyers, others labourers; there were conquerors and captives, farmers and fishermen, scholars and shepherds, priests, prophets, poets and a physician. It describes the work of God in the affairs of men. Its scope covers time past, present, future and on into eternity. The Bible is divided into the Old and New Testaments. The Old looks forward to the coming of Christ; the New describes and applies his coming.

The Bible never glosses over the sins and failures of its greatest heroes. We even read of murder, lying, adultery, swearing, pride and bitter contentions in their lives.

Every area of life is covered including fear, love, envy, greed, family life, slavery, violence, war and peace, exile, wilderness experiences, sea life, dreams, songs, wit and music.

The Bible itself claims to be God's message to man. In the Old Testament alone we read phrases like 'the Lord spoke' or 'thus says the Lord' over 2,600 times. The Bible asserts that:

All the Bible is inspired, or God-breathed

All Scripture is given by inspiration of God, and is profitable for doctrine, for reproof, for correction, for instruction in righteousness that the man of God may be complete, thoroughly equipped for every good work.[1]

The writers themselves were inspired by God

For prophecy never came by the will of man, but holy men of God spoke as they were moved by the Holy Spirit.[2]

Every individual letter is inspired by God

Now to Abraham and his seed were the promises made. He does not say, 'And to seeds,' as of many, but as of one, 'And to your seed,' who is Christ.[3]

Here the argument is being made on the basis of one letter.

Every 'jot or tittle' (that is, even the smallest letter or mark in Hebrew writing) is inspired by God

For assuredly, I say to you, till heaven and earth pass away, one jot or one tittle will by no means pass from the law till all is fulfilled.[4]

The clear-cut claim of the Bible is that each of the sixty-six books—each chapter, each word, and every letter—is given by inspiration of God, and so the Bible is trustworthy and sufficient. It is truly human, yet totally divine.

2. It is old, yet new

A unique feature of the Bible is its agelessness, shown on the one hand by the remarkable recording of future events long before (sometimes hundreds of years before) they happened in history, and on the other by the continual relevancy and application of truths written down centuries ago in a culture that, to us, is quite alien.

Some wish to dismiss the Bible as fable. How, then, do they explain the total accuracy of literally hundreds of prophecies? How was the future so clearly foretold? Who but God, who inhabits eternity, can see what lies ahead? These are not vague predictions such as those of Nostradamus or a fortune-teller's hit-and-miss generalisations, but detailed descriptions of forthcoming events. The statistical probability of their chance fulfilment is too great to be even considered. Prophecies concerning countries, cities, peoples, individuals, the person and work of Christ, the progress of the Church, the times in which we live and the end of the world are written in detail throughout the Bible. All, apart from those concerning the end of the world, have been fulfilled in intricate detail. Some, such as the return of the Jews to their own country and the taking again of their capital city, Jerusalem, have happened in comparatively recent years. (Incidentally, it is surely harder to predict the future than to describe the past. If, then, God accurately foretells the future, can we not trust him in the accounts of history we read in the Bible?) Repeatedly God, a God of love, warns various groups of people of impending judgement if they do not turn from their wicked ways. These love-based warnings became some of the most amazing prophecies fulfilled; they were fulfilled in such a way that none could deny their authenticity.

Neither the birth of Buddha, Mohammed nor any of the many gurus was predicted; but the birth, life, teaching, work, death, resurrection, and forthcoming reign, of Christ were all carefully prophesied hundreds of years before his incarnation. Again we ask, who but a timeless God could see the future and cause to have written down so precisely what would happen? Interestingly, of course, the Old Testament is basically a Jewish book, and therefore Christians cannot be open to the charge of 'tampering' with or changing these prophecies. Every Jewish scholar would vouch for the accuracy of the Old Testament scriptures we shall quote. It remains the world's most translated book as well as the world's best seller. In the first five books of the Bible alone, phrases such as 'the Lord spoke', 'the Lord commanded' or 'the word of the Lord' occur nearly seven hundred times; in the complete Old Testament, as we have seen, over 2,600 times. The Old Testament saturates the New, which itself fulfils the Old. Let us then look at three groups (from the dozens we could have chosen) of these prophecies concerning:

A specific place

In 588 BC the prophet Ezekiel said:

> Therefore thus says the Lord God: 'Behold, I am against you, O Tyre, and will cause many nations to come up against you, as the sea causes its waves to come up. And they shall destroy the walls of Tyre and break down her towers; I will also scrape her dust from her, and make her like the top of a rock.' For thus says the Lord God: 'Behold, I will bring against Tyre from the north Nebuchadnezzar king of Babylon, king of kings, with horses, with chariots, and with horsemen, and an army with many people. He will slay with the sword your daughter villages in the fields; he will heap up a siege-mound against you, build a wall against

you, and raise a defence against you. They will plunder your riches and pillage your merchandise; they will break down your walls and destroy your pleasant houses; they will lay your stones, your timber, and your soil in the midst of the water. I will make you like the top of a rock; you shall be a place for spreading nets, and you shall never be rebuilt, for I the Lord have spoken,' says the Lord God. 'I will make you a terror, and you shall be no more; though you are sought for, you will never be found again,' says the Lord God.[5]

The prediction states that Nebuchadnezzar would destroy the mainland city of Tyre. Many nations would be against the city and eventually make her a flat bare rock; only fishermen would spread nets over the site and debris would be thrown into the water. The city would never be rebuilt and never found again.

Three years after the prophecy Nebuchadnezzar laid siege to mainland Tyre. As the *Encyclopaedia Britannica* states, 'After a thirteen-year siege (585–573 BC) by Nebuchadnezzar II Tyre made terms and acknowledged Babylonian suzerainty.' However, when Nebuchadnezzar broke down the gates, the city was almost empty. Most of the people had moved by ship to an island about half a mile from the coast and had fortified a city there. In 573 the mainland city was destroyed.

The island city, however, remained powerful until 332 BC. When the inhabitants refused to surrender to him, Alexander the Great totally demolished the old mainland city and with the debris built a causeway two hundred feet wide to reach the island city, which he then captured and sacked. Today the old city of Tyre is still as a bare, flat rock used only by fishermen to dry their nets; the new city is down the coast from the original site. The biblical prophecy was fulfilled exactly as predicted.

A specific person

The Old Testament contains over three hundred references to Christ's coming. His birth, life, death, resurrection and influences are prophesied in detail.

About 400 BC Malachi wrote:

> 'Behold, I send my messenger, and he will prepare the way before me. And the Lord, whom you seek, will suddenly come to his temple, even the Messenger of the covenant, in whom you delight. Behold, he is coming,' says the Lord of hosts.[6]

This was fulfilled in the coming of John the Baptist:

> John came baptizing in the wilderness and preaching a baptism of repentance for the remission of sins.[7]

Isaiah around 700 BC prophesied the virgin birth of Jesus:

> Therefore the Lord himself will give you a sign: Behold, the virgin shall conceive and bear a Son, and shall call his name Immanuel.[8]

Matthew describes its fulfilment:

> And did not know her till she had brought forth her first-born Son. And he called his name Jesus.[9]

Micah (*c*. 700 BC) even states the place of Jesus' birth:

> But you, Bethlehem Ephrathah, though you are little among the thousands of Judah, yet out of you shall come forth to me the one to be ruler in Israel, whose goings forth have been from of old, from everlasting.[10]

Isaiah (*c*. 700 BC) described Jesus and his royal descent:

For unto us a Child is born, unto us a Son is given; and the government will be upon his shoulder. And his name will be called Wonderful, Counsellor, Mighty God, Everlasting Father, Prince of Peace. Of the increase of his government and peace there will be no end, upon the throne of David and over his kingdom, to order it and establish it with judgment and justice from that time forward, even for ever. The zeal of the Lord of hosts will perform this.[11]

Zechariah (*c.* 500 BC) describes Jesus' entry into Jerusalem:

Rejoice greatly, O daughter of Zion! Shout, O daughter of Jerusalem! Behold, your King is coming to you; he is just and having salvation, lowly and riding on a donkey, a colt, the foal of a donkey.[12]

We read of Jesus' betrayal:

Even my own familiar friend in whom I trusted, who ate my bread, has lifted up his heel against me.[13]

Written about 1,000 BC and in Zechariah:

'If it is agreeable to you, give me my wages; and if not, refrain.' So they weighed out for my wages thirty pieces of silver. And the Lord said to me, 'Throw it to the potter'— that princely price they set on me. So I took the thirty pieces of silver and threw them into the house of the Lord for the potter.[14]

The death of Christ, which is the central theme of the Bible, and is God's means of bringing us to himself, was prophesied hundreds of years before it happened and indeed before crucifixion was devised. Zechariah wrote in about 500 BC:

'Awake, O sword, against my Shepherd, against the man who is my companion,' says the Lord of hosts. 'Strike the

Shepherd, and the sheep will be scattered; then I will turn my hand against the little ones.'[15]

And I will pour on the house of David and on the inhabitants of Jerusalem the Spirit of grace and supplication; then they will look on me whom they have pierced; they will mourn for him as one mourns for his only son, and grieve for him as one grieves for a firstborn.[16]

Isaiah (*c.* 700 BC) graphically wrote concerning the awful events of Christ's crucifixion:

Just as many were astonished at you, so his visage was marred more than any man, and his form more than the sons of men.[17]

Who has believed our report? And to whom has the arm of the Lord been revealed? For he shall grow up before him as a tender plant, and as a root out of dry ground. He has no form or comeliness; and when we see him, there is no beauty that we should desire him. He is despised and rejected by men, a man of sorrows and acquainted with grief. And we hid, as it were, our faces from him; he was despised, and we did not esteem him. Surely he has borne our griefs and carried our sorrows; yet we esteemed him stricken, smitten by God and afflicted. But he was wounded for our transgressions, he was bruised for our iniquities; the chastisement for our peace was upon him, and by his stripes we are healed. All we like sheep have gone astray; we have turned, every one, to his own way; and the Lord has laid on him the iniquity of us all.... And they made his grave with the wicked—but with the rich at his death, because he had done no violence, nor was any deceit in his mouth. Yet it pleased the Lord to bruise him; he has put him to grief. When you make his soul an offering for sin, he shall see his seed, he shall prolong his days, and the pleasure of the Lord shall prosper in his hand. He shall see the travail of his soul, and be satisfied. By his knowledge my righteous servant shall justify many, for he shall bear their iniquities. Therefore I will divide him a portion with the great, and he shall divide the spoil with the strong, because he poured out his soul unto death, and he was numbered with the transgressors, and he bore the sin of many, and made intercession for the transgressors.[18]

David described the agony of crucifixion, the gambling for Christ's garments and how no bones of Jesus would be broken:

I am poured out like water, and all my bones are out of joint; my heart is like wax; it has melted within me. My strength is dried up like a potsherd [broken pottery], and my tongue clings to my jaws; you have brought me to the dust of death. For dogs have surrounded me; the assembly of the wicked has enclosed me. They pierced my hands and my feet; I can count all my bones. They look and stare at me. They divide my garments among them, and for my clothing they cast lots.[19]

He guards all his bones; not one of them is broken.[20]

They also gave me gall for my food, and for my thirst they gave me vinegar to drink.[21]

As Dale Rhoton says, 'To the open-minded person the conclusion is inescapable. These prophecies must have come from God and therefore what they said must have been true.'[22]

Indeed! Let any atheist try to explain such prophecies! They are clear evidence of the Bible being the word of God.

A specific people

The Bible says much about the Jewish people. The 'father of the Jews' was Abraham. To him God promised and prophesied the Israelites' four hundred years of bondage in Egypt followed by their return to the land he would give them.[23] In the book of Deuteronomy[24] God warned of the disasters that would come upon the nation of Israel if they deliberately disobeyed his will. He spoke specifically of the Jewish dispersal and persecution. Centuries later the prophet Jeremiah pleaded with God's people to turn from their sins. They continually rejected God's warnings through him. Jeremiah wrote a letter, which stated that for seventy years the people would be in captivity in Babylon. This is exactly what eventually happened, in fulfilment of specific prophecies.[25]

The Bible also makes prophecies and predictions that are in reality promises concerning God's people today. In each continent and country there are men and women, young and old, who are trusting Christ as Lord and Saviour. They are in a real sense God's special people.[26] Knowing Christ proves not just academically but experientially the truth and reality of such statements as:

> Ho! Everyone who thirsts, come to the waters; and you who have no money, come, buy and eat. Yes, come, buy wine and milk without money and without price. Why do you spend money for what is not bread, and your wages for what does not satisfy? Listen diligently to me; and eat what is good, and let your soul delight itself in abundance. Incline your ear, and come to me. Hear, and your soul shall live; and I will make an everlasting covenant with you—the sure mercies of David.[27]

> I will give you a new heart and put a new spirit within you; I will take the heart of stone out of your flesh and give you a heart of flesh. I will put my Spirit within you and cause you to walk in my statutes, and you will keep my judgments and do them. I will deliver you from all your uncleannesses.[28]

> In him was life, and the life was the light of men. But as many as received him, to them he gave the right to become children of God, even to those who believe in his name: who were born, not of blood, nor of the will of the flesh, nor of the will of man, but of God. And of his fullness we have all received, and grace for grace.[29]

I have come that they may have life, and that they may have it more abundantly.[30]

Therefore, if anyone is in Christ, he is a new creation; old things have passed away; behold, all things have become new.[31]

At this point, I would like to stress that Christians are not anti-science. Far from it! Science is the systematic pursuit of knowledge and, of course, discovering aspects of truth is perfectly consistent with Christian experience. History verifies this as so many scientists, such as Sir Isaac Newton, Robert Boyle, Sir James Simpson and Michael Faraday, were practising Christians.

The trouble is that we have cloaked the scientist with a mantle of infallibility, but a true scientist is known by his confession of ignorance. For example, Johannes Kepler, who discovered that planetary orbits are elliptical, reflected, 'O God, I am thinking Thy thoughts after Thee.' Isaac Newton said: 'I do not know what I may appear to the world, but to myself I seem to have been only like a boy playing on the sea-shore, and diverting myself in now and then finding a smoother pebble or a prettier shell than ordinary, whilst the great ocean of truth lay all undiscovered before me.'

The inventor Thomas Eddison once said, 'I do not know one millionth part of one per cent about anything.'

Edward Jenner, the discoverer of the benefits of vaccination, said, 'I do not wonder that men are grateful to me, but I am surprised that they do not feel gratitude to God for thus making me a medium of good.'

After all, scientists cannot explain the source of kindness, love, beauty, friendship or fairness. They cannot say where we are going, or why it is that mankind universally demonstrates a spiritual dimension and a desire to worship.

However, the question, 'Why believe, when we have science?' is still a common sentiment of many. The notion that the first book of the Bible, Genesis, is to be discarded as myth is popular dogma.

The book of Genesis is arguably the most important book ever to be written. It is the foundation to the world's best seller, the Bible. It is the basis of the most influential piece of literature to have been produced. If the first thirty-four verses of Genesis are true, then atheism, agnosticism, materialism, hedonism, existentialism, polytheism and pantheism are all invalidated. If Genesis is true, the most pressing need of man is to find out more about the Creator God who made us and to whom we are responsible.

Science does not contradict the Bible, nor does the Bible contradict science. There are, however, scientific theories (rather than proven facts) and misguided biblical interpretations that may give the impression that there are contradictions. Perhaps limited knowledge leads to limited theories upon which many feel they can build a case and a life that excuses them from trust in God.

Take, for example, the two areas of controversy relating to the creation of the world and miraculous acts. Theories seeking to describe scientifically the age of the world and how it began are often thought to prove the Bible to be untrue. However, there are other explanations.

Some have suggested that perhaps the six days of Genesis chapter 1 really represent long periods of time. 'After all,' they argue, 'are not a thousand years as a day in the sight of God?'

However, Genesis is a historical rather than a poetical book. Why then should this part alone be described as symbolic?

In Genesis chapter 1 we read of the chronological order of creation, then in chapter 2, man is the focal point of attention and the centre point of creation. All creation is seen in relation to the pinnacle of creation.

Adam and Eve were made with 'apparent age'. They were not created as little babies, but rather as adults. Interestingly, the plants, trees, fish and animals were likewise made with the physical appearance of maturity. There has been much questioning about the age of the earth. Perhaps it, too, was made with apparent age?

In the early chapters of Genesis we read of the origin of the universe, of order, of the solar system, of the atmosphere and hydrosphere, of life, of man, of marriage, of evil, of language, of government, of culture, of nations, of religion, of music, of poetry, of communities and of a chosen people.

If we truly grasped the greatness of the 'God-ness' of God, our question would not be, 'How could God create such a complex world in such a short time?', but 'Why did he take six days creating something that could have been made in an instant?'

In all the world there is the seal of a great and glorious Creator of such marvellous things. I once saw a cartoon that expresses the wonder of the beauty of creation. It showed two monks surveying some marvellous scenery in the distance. One was saying to the other, 'I like his use of green in the bottom left-hand corner!' Nature testifies to the glory of God. It is reasonable to believe that behind designs there must be a Designer, behind something made there must be a Maker, behind creation there must be a Creator.

But the sceptic will also question the miracles. Again, though, if God is truly God he is well able to intervene, even if the result does not act in accordance with the usual observable laws of nature. Here is the clue to overcoming what has been a problem to some. A scientist is limited in being able only to explain what he actually sees. If God is taken into account, the explanation and outcome may be very different.

For example, given a piece of bread and asked to describe how it was made, a scientist would naturally detail how the corn was planted in the earth, its growth, harvesting, grinding, mixing with other ingredients and finally its baking in the oven. Of course that would be fine, unless, that is, something remarkably exceptional had happened. Suppose, instead, the particular piece of bread under examination was one that had been picked up after Jesus had taken five loaves and two fishes, given thanks, then broken and distributed them to feed the five thousand, as described in Matthew chapter 14, verses 13 to 21. We read that twelve baskets of left-overs were gathered (showing, incidentally, how much Christ abhorred waste). If the piece of bread in question was one of these fragments, or from the incident a little later when Jesus fed four thousand with seven loaves and a few fish (read Matthew 15:29–39), the scientist would have been wrong in his analysis and description, because he failed to take into account the supernatural hand of the Creator.

The scientist would make a similar and understandable mistake if he described the birth, growth, catching and grilling of the fish, if in fact this too was the product of miraculous and instantaneous multiplication by the Lord Jesus. Or again, suppose wine were given to a professional wine-taster or a scientist to describe its country of origin and vintage. As he swilled it round in the glass, smelled and tasted it, he could perhaps describe this mature-tasting drink, perhaps even locating its country of origin and pin-pointing one of the finest vineyards in that land. However, this time, far from being the natural product of grapes that had undergone years of fermentation, it was made in an instant. Jesus was attending a wedding feast at Cana in Galilee, as described in John 2:1–11. The wine ran out, but Jesus commanded that six large earthenware pots be filled with water. As the chief steward tasted the drink, he found it was the best of wine. Knowledge of the presence of the Creator would change the whole outlook on the wine

itself. It was made in an instant rather than the long
process that appeared to be the more obvious method.

If the Bible is as it claims to be, the word of God, then
we would expect to read of the works of God. If these
were within the realm of normal human experience then
one would rightly question whether they were a demonstration of God or merely of man. It is surely reasonable
to expect God to work in ways that are beyond human
comprehension. This does not disprove the Bible but
demonstrates the infinity of God and the limitations of
our finite minds and scientific pursuit.

3. It is a library, yet one book

Most books are the product of an individual author. The
Bible, in contrast, was written by more than forty
authors over sixteen centuries. They came from four
cultures and wrote in three languages (Hebrew, Aramaic
and Greek) on three continents. For example, the old
man Moses wrote in the wilderness in Hebrew, fifteen
hundred years before the apostle John, incarcerated in
prison on the isle of Patmos, wrote his book of the
Revelation in Greek. It matters not whether the authors
penned their writings in a nomadic tent, a beautiful
palace, a dungeon, in the midst of battle, or out in the
fields. Each sentence is part of an overall picture that is
united and complete. History, poetry, prophecy, letters
and Gospel records combine to form a revelation that is
a perfect blueprint from God to us.

One would expect a clash of culture, thought, philo-
sophy and belief; however, there is absolute harmony.
Doctrines, outlook and even the use of words blend
together perfectly.

Unity in doctrine

As soon as Adam and Eve sinned, they are seen hiding
from God, who took the initiative in searching for them.

Whereas most other major world religions are alike in that they are all to do with humanity struggling to find a way back to God, biblical religion is unique; it is about God coming to seek and to save us who are lost. The theme of the Bible is redemption (God buying back sinful, lost mankind). In the Old Testament it is prophesied and pictured: in the New it is accomplished.

Think for a moment of this volume written over a period of sixteen hundred years by forty different men, but consistently speaking so eloquently of the holiness of God, the sinfulness of man, the redemption Christ died to buy for men and women, as well as the promise of spiritual life on earth and in eternity for those who by faith come to know God. Without collaboration these authors were 'of a mind' as they wrote of God's dealings with them.

What do I do if I recognise my sin and guilt and long for it to be removed? Am I really to believe that visiting Mecca, Rome, the River Ganges or some other 'holy' place is sufficient to please God? Will turning over a new leaf and seeking not to sin again make up for my past deficiencies? Does God merely desire that I become an automaton, submissive to my religious rituals? The Bible teaches another and better way altogether.

Sin always brings death: either the death of the sinner or the death of a sacrifice or substitute. In Old Testament days God ordained that a sinner was to take a spotless male lamb to the Jewish priest. This was in itself an act of confession. The sinner and the Jewish priest would lay a hand on the head of the lamb. Then the lamb would die, its blood shed for sin. Thousands upon thousands died in this way, not because God loves bloodshed, but to reveal the horrible seriousness of sin and to portray God's ultimate remedy for sin in Christ.

The shadowy picture of animal sacrifice in the Old Testament was eventually to be done away with completely. In the fullness of time a baby was born. The angel said, 'Call his name Jesus for he shall save his people from their sin.' There was only one way he could do that; he was to die as a sacrifice and a substitute for the world's sin. No wonder when John the Baptist saw Jesus, he pointed the crowds to him saying, 'Behold the Lamb of God who takes away the sin of the world!'[32]

Christ eventually was to die as the innocent, pure, male lamb. He took away the sin that no animal could take. He carried on himself all past and future sin. He was completing what Jewish writers and readers had eagerly looked for over many centuries. No wonder he was to cry on the cross, 'It is finished.' He was speaking of this completed work of redemption.

Paul wrote that, 'In him we have redemption through his blood'[33] and Peter said we are 'not redeemed with corruptible things, like silver or gold...but with the precious blood of Christ, as of a lamb without blemish and without spot'.[34]

The very last book in the Bible foretells a theme in heaven for all those who have trusted in the finished work of Christ: 'Worthy is the Lamb who was slain.'[35]

The universality and seriousness of sin, as well as the necessity of being redeemed by the Lamb of God, are examples of the oneness in theme that exists throughout the Bible.

Unity in outlook

Using imagery, symbolism, logic, oratory, poetry and reasoning, there is a spiritual tone throughout the Bible that describes the pathos and trauma of a godless society set on rejecting God and his commands; yet it produces profound hope solidly based on the work and promises of God. For example:

> My tears have been my food day and night, while they continually say to me, 'Where is your God?' Why are you cast down, O my soul? And why are you disquieted within me? Hope in God; for I shall yet praise him, the help of my

countenance and my God.'[36]

Moses, five hundred years before the psalm was written, and the disciples, one thousand years after, had the same attitude; namely, a deep pessimism at the sinfulness of man overtaken by total optimism, knowing the overriding and triumphant power of God's goodness.

Unity in words

Bible scholars have long been aware of the miraculous unity in the word of God, and hence have often studied individual words and their use throughout the Bible. As with the doctrines, there are many examples, but here let us take the example of the word 'thorns'.

God cursed the earth after man had first sinned. The Lord said, 'Both thorns and thistles it shall bring forth for you.'[37] So thorns are the result of sin and the curse of God.

Later when Abraham was stopped from sacrificing his son Isaac, God told him instead to sacrifice a ram caught in a thicket, or thorn bush.[38] The sacrifice was caught by that which represents sin—the thorns.

When the Lord Jesus Christ was to be crucified he had wedged on his head a crown made with thorns. The mark of sin was now crowning the Saviour of the world. After all, that is what the cross was all about.

Although the Bible is a collection of books, it is actually one book with one theme revealing the one and only way to the one God.

4. It is ignored, yet influential

Although the Bible is widely distributed and easily available in the West, it is a characteristic of recent generations in some countries that they are ignoring or attacking it.

Most people feel they have a smattering of knowledge, but in reality this is limited. Religious cults capitalise on this by quoting their selective verses, thus giving the impression that they know their Bible. Some who go to church have little real grasp of biblical truths and fail to allow their lives to be governed by them.

The Bible has been read by more people and translated into more languages than any other book. It has survived through time, persecution and criticism as the anvil upon which many hammers have had their day but been eventually discarded as ineffective. For example, Tom Paine wrote one of the first anti-Bible books, entitled *The Age of Reason*. He concludes with words to this effect, 'I have been through the Bible like a woodman going through trees with his axe. Let the priests try and put the trees back on the stumps if they can.' This was written, of course, many years ago. Tom Paine is dead and forgotten; yet the Bible not only lives but goes forward with growing influence. The 'priests' did not put the trees back on their stumps; the trees were never severed. Tom Paine was wrong.

In 1874 the Scriptures were under severe attack by critics, and John W. Haley published a defence entitled *Alleged Discrepancies of the Bible*. In the preface he wrote:

> Finally, let it be remembered that the Bible is neither dependent upon nor affected by the success or failure of my book. Whatever may become of the latter, whatever may be the verdict passed upon it by an intelligent public, the Bible will stand. In the ages yet to be, when its present assailants and defenders are mouldering in the dust, and when our very names are forgotten, [God's word] will be, as it has been during the centuries past, the guide and solace of millions.

My experience is that those who attack Scripture most are those who know it least. Those who accuse it as being full of contradictions have picked up second-hand arguments and not checked to find the straightforward answers that are in the context of the passage.

Gladstone, the illustrious nineteenth century prime minister, wrote a book on the Bible entitled, *The Impregnable Rock of Holy Scripture*. When Churchill read it, he commented that he had no reason to disagree. Such men are not hoodwinked, nor are the millions who have staked their lives and eternities upon its teachings and promises.

The Bible may be ignored by many, but its power is unleashed upon those who read it.

A Yorkshire miner was converted after reading the words: 'For God so loved the world that he gave his only begotten Son' on the back of a bus ticket. Presumably the next part of the famous verse found in John chapter 3 verse 16 was on the next bus ticket! A London journalist trusted Christ after reading the words, 'Christ died for our sins' imprinted on a cheap ball-point pen! Neither of these men had any religious background, but God's word, the Bible, spoke powerfully to them both.

Professor Michael Clarkson heads up the Department of Veterinary Parasitology at Liverpool University. He was brought up in an atheistic background and as he started his studies he would have described himself as an agnostic. Intrigued by the title of a lecture being organised by Christians at the University, he went to listen to a man speak on 'The Impossibility of Agnosticism'. He was not convinced; but took up the challenge of the speaker, who said he would give to anyone who wanted one, a booklet, which he guaranteed would lead to the conversion of anyone reading it with an open mind. Sceptically, Michael Clarkson took a copy—it was John's Gospel. Weeks later, during the Christmas vacation, he read it. In the silence of his home, he became convinced of its truths and received Christ as his Saviour and Lord.

The Bible's influence is second to none. Adolf Hitler wrote in the preface to *Mein Kampf*: 'I know that fewer people are won over by the written word than by the spoken word and that every great movement on this earth owes its growth to great speakers and not to great writers.' As far as the Bible is concerned, Hitler was wrong. When a person starts to read, the power of God is let loose as the Holy Spirit takes hold of the Holy Bible and applies it with almighty power to transform unholy lives.

In both the joys and deepest struggles of life the Bible has been a source of inward strength to so many.

If Alexander Graham Bell was the improver of the telephone, Philip Reiss was its inventor. At the end of his life, he referred to the 'Holy Scriptures' saying, 'The Lord has bestowed more good upon me than I have known how to ask of him. The Lord has helped me hitherto; he will help yet further.'

William Wilberforce, whose labours brought about the abolition of slavery in the British Empire, wrote: 'My judgement...rests altogether on the word of God,' and, 'If you read the Scriptures with earnest prayer...and a sincere desire for discovering the truth and obeying it when known, I cannot doubt of your attaining it.'

Woodrow Wilson, the US statesman and president said, 'When you have read the Bible, you will know that it is the word of God, because you will have found it the key to your own heart, your own happiness and your own duty.'

The great nineteenth century American preacher, Henry Ward Beecher wrote, 'The Bible is God's chart for you to steer by, to keep you from the bottom of the sea, and to show you where the harbour is and how to reach it without running on rocks or bars.'

Bible translators continue their relentless task of translating the Scriptures into every language, because they know the power of the word of God to change and improve not only individuals but culture and behaviour. The Bible gives the one remedy to the bondage of guilt and sin.

Our own culture has been permeated by the truths of the Bible, truths that have affected our democracy, our legal system, our freedoms, our arts, music, literature, and architecture. Such is the influence of the Bible.

5. I have read it, yet it read me

I don't know that I would have read a 170-page biography of a Middle-Eastern pastor who lived during the first part of the twentieth century—except that my mother wrote it! I not only read it, but loved it. Knowing the author made all the difference.

The Bible is not like a Shakespearian play, intended to be read merely as literature. Rather, it is a book that is spiritually understood. It has a divine author, one who is reaching out in love to lost men and women. Through its words God speaks. Praying and asking God to teach us as we read is the way to benefit from the word of God.

As a person reads he discovers that God sees us just as we are. So many won't read it because they know they are guilty of the sins it condemns. The Bible condemns every sin and condones none; it accuses all and excuses none; it abuses human reason and exalts God's revelation. It points us away from ourselves to Christ. It is the word of God and therefore ought to be read daily until it becomes a delight. Why not read it yourself? Start in the New Testament, say with John's Gospel. Don't use notes or commentaries, but just let God himself teach you as you read.

Notes

1. 2 Timothy 3:16,17.

 2. 2 Peter 1:21.
 3. Galatians 3:16.
 4. Matthew 5:18.
 5. Ezekiel 26:3,4,7,8,12,14,21.
 6. Malachi 3:1.
 7. Mark 1:4.
 8. Isaiah 7:14.
 9. Matthew 1:25.
10. Micah 5:2.
11. Isaiah 9:6,7.
12. Zechariah 9:9.
13. Psalm 41:9.
14. Zechariah 11:12,13.
15. Zechariah 13:7.
16. Zechariah 12:10.
17. Isaiah 52:14.
18. Isaiah 53:1–6,9–12.
19. Psalm 22:14–18.
20. Psalm 34:20.
21. Psalm 69:21.
22. Dale Rhoton, *The Logic of Faith* (STL Books, 1978, p.72).
23. Genesis 15:12–16.
24. Deuteronomy 28:15 and following verses (ff.); 64ff.
25. Jeremiah 29:10ff; Daniel 9:2.
26. 1 Peter 2:9.
27. Isaiah 55:1–3.
28. Ezekiel 36:26,27,29.
29. John 1:4,12,13,16.
30. John 10:10b.
31. 2 Corinthians 5:17.
32. John 1:29.
33. Ephesians 1:7.
34. 1 Peter 1:18,19.
35. Revelation 5:12.
36. Psalm 42:3,11.
37. Genesis 3:18.
38. Genesis 22:13.

2

Why Believe the Devil Is the Enemy of God?

Jesus said: The ruler of this world [Satan] is coming,
and he has nothing in me. . . . be of good cheer, I have
overcome the world.
John 14:30; 16:33

A friend of mine was visiting a Church Missionary Society hospital in Kenya. While being taken round and introduced to some of the patients, he met an African whose arms were just bandaged stumps. Enquiring about what had happened, he was told that the patient was a village witch-doctor. His power was such that if anyone crossed him, he would simply point at his enemy and before the day was over it was known that he would be dead. The villagers had been in such fear of the witch-doctor's power that one night they banded together, raided his hut, chopped off his hands so he could never again point, and took him to the missionary hospital. Although they took drastic measures against the witch-doctor, they knew well enough the reality of Satan's power.

The devil is not the red man carrying a pitchfork, seeking to do little bits of mischief wherever he can, as often caricatured by the cartoonist. Neither is he the all-powerful undefeatable foe that some see him as. We shall see later in this chapter that Jesus has already won the victory over Satan by his work on the cross.[1] It is also true that God gives Christians weapons not only to resist Satan but to send him fleeing.[2] At this point, however, I want to make it very clear that the Bible says two things about everything that is associated with the devil, be it sorcery, fortune-telling by any means whatsoever (including astrology), spiritualism, the occult and powers of darkness: first, they are real and are to be taken seriously, and secondly they are wrong, hated by God and therefore to be avoided. The Bible also records the disastrous consequences of those who choose to ignore God's commands.

King Saul, whose career started so well, ended his days by consulting a medium. Earlier he had ordered that the land be cleared of such people, but eventually he was to ask, 'Please, conduct a seance for me, and bring up for me the one I shall name to you.'[3] His contact with the witch of Endor was as a direct result of his separation from God.[4] A few days' later Saul was to die in battle.

Centuries later, Isaiah had to contend with a whole nation that was set on seeking mediums and wizards.[5] Eventually the nation, having turned its back on God, was overrun by enemy armies.

In more recent years interest in the occult has been greater than one at first might imagine. Peter Anderson in his book *Talk of the Devil*[6] mentions some of the more influential characters who have had such involvement.

Mary Baker Eddy, founder of Christian Science, worked as a professional medium in New York for many years. Joseph Smith, originator of the Mormon faith, claims to have received his 'revelations' from a spirit that he knew as 'Moroni'. Emmanuel Swedenborg, whose followers founded the churches of the 'New Jerusalem', claimed to have communicated with the 'dead' on many occasions.

Dr Carl Jung, the famous Swiss psychologist, also possessed unusual occult powers and often had horoscopes cast for his patients. He claimed to have a spirit guide named

'Philemon', and often spoke with him. In fact, Dr Jung won his doctorate with a thesis on the subject of the occult.

Abraham Lincoln consulted with a medium over his 'Emancipation Proclamation'. Jeane Dixon, the American clairvoyant, claims that on more than one occasion President Roosevelt invited her to predict for him. Even Sir Winston Churchill said that there had been times when he had turned to the 'spirit of the glass' for help in his hour of need.

Astrologers were engaged by several governments during World War II and many of these produced astrological calculations for propaganda purposes. In Nazi Germany, Himmler employed a corps of mediums in the service of the SS.

British mediums have on occasions offered their services to the police, and one well known Dutch clairvoyant has already been consulted by seven European police chiefs in murder investigations.

Richard Wurmbrand has argued that Marx was in fact a Satanist.[7]

Today in our secular society well-known book clubs promote authors and books that revel in the supernatural; high-street bookshops sell tarot cards; toy shops sell games like 'Dungeons and Dragons', 'Horoscope', 'Mystic Eye', and ouija boards; cinemas and television have shown a whole string of films about the supernatural with its sadism, sordidness and sensuality. Horoscopes appear in newspapers, magazines, television and radio programmes and therefore in the thinking of the general public. Mediums fill town halls and seaside theatres as they publicly conduct seances and tell fortunes, and well-known entertainers encourage their followers to emulate them by publicly sharing their involvement in the occult.

Sad as all this is, it does not take the Christian by surprise. The apostle Paul said that a sign of 'the last days' would be people departing 'from the faith, giving heed to deceiving spirits and doctrines of demons'.[8]

Who is the devil?

The Bible describes the devil as a spiritual being who
has intelligence, power and authority. He is the source of
all evil and sin. That does not mean that we are not
responsible for our actions. 'The devil made me do it' is
no excuse—you did it!

In the Bible he is called the destroyer,[9] the deceiver,[10]
a liar and the father of lies,[11] a murderer,[12] the prince of
the power of the air,[13] and the serpent.[14] He is likened to
a roaring lion seeking people to devour.[15] He (not 'leisure, pleasure or treasure') is called the god of this age.[16]

Jesus likened him to a thief who comes to steal, to kill
and to destroy.[17] Suicidal thoughts in our minds, destruc-
tive forces in Christian work and divisive influences in
churches are surely of the devil. Certainly Satan attacks
Christians and buffets them.[18] He is described as hinder-
ing Christian work, as Paul found when he desired to
visit the believers in Thessalonica.[19] The Greek word
rendered 'hindered' in this verse literally means 'to
break up the road along the way'.

Christ warned that in the last days Satan would perform signs and wonders—even 'great signs and lying
wonders'. In fact, although Jesus himself performed
signs, he often warned against Satan's counterfeiting of
them.[20]

If there is no devil, who inspired Adolf Hitler to
systematically exterminate the Jews and bring about suffering for millions? Who was behind a terrorist who
packed explosives over his body then drove a lorry full of
explosives into an American camp in Beirut, blasting
himself and one hundred marines into eternity? Who is
behind those who continue to carry out repeated atroci-
ties in Ulster? Who has brought the world to the brink of
self-destruction? Who has led millions to ignore their
Creator and live with no thought of God or eternity?

The same point has been made rather more amusingly
in a poem by Alfred J. Hough:

Men don't believe in the devil now, as their fathers
    used to do;
They've forced the door of the broadest creed to let
    his majesty through.
There isn't a print of his cloven foot or fiery dart from
    his bow
To be found on earth or air today, for the world has
    voted it so.
Who dogs the steps of the toiling saint and digs the
    pits for his feet?
Who sows the tares in the fields of time whenever God
    sows the wheat?
The devil is voted not to be, and of course, the thing is
    true;
But who is doing the kind of work that the devil alone
    can do?
We are told that he doesn't go about as a roaring lion
    now;
But whom shall we hold responsible for the everlast-
    ing row
To be heard in home, in Church and state, to the
    earth's remotest bound,
If the devil by unanimous vote is nowhere to be
    found?
Won't someone step to the front forthwith and make
    their bow and show
How the frauds and crimes of a single day spring up?
We want to know!
The devil was fairly voted out, and of course, the
    devil's gone;
But simple people would like to know who carried the
    business on?[21]

God is a Trinity—there is a plurality of personality in
the Godhead—the Father, the Son and the Holy Spirit.
The devil is the enemy of each member of the Trinity.

The devil—the enemy of the Father

We do not know all the details of the early work and fall of the devil. However, he was obviously a beautiful, created angel who wanted to be as God. Isaiah[22] fills in some detail:

> How you are fallen from heaven, O Lucifer, son of the morning! How you are cut down to the ground, you who weakéned the nations! For you have said in your heart: 'I will ascend into heaven, I will exalt my throne above the stars of God; I will also sit on the mount of the congregation on the farthest sides of the north; I will ascend above the heights of the clouds, I will be like the Most High.' Yet you shall be brought down to Sheol, to the lowest depths of the Pit.

Pride filled the devil. As we see in the above quotation, five times he said 'I will', rather than 'Thy will be done'.

Having been cast out of heaven to the hell prepared for him and his angels, he then set to work to destroy the wonder of creation. He approached Adam and Eve questioning the word of God, adding to it, taking from it and changing it (a pattern of operation the devil still follows today). The devil sought to substitute a lie for the truth of God's word. All that radiated the glory of God, the devil sought to tarnish. Adam and Eve lost their purity and their paradise.

Probably the oldest book in the Bible is Job. It tells the story of a godly man whose family and business were blessed of God. The devil, the supreme cynic, attributed wrong motives to Job's apparent godliness saying:

> Does Job fear God for nothing? Have you not made a hedge around him, around his household, and around all that he has on every side? You have blessed the work of his hands, and his possessions have increased in the land. But now,

stretch out your hand and touch all that he has, and he will surely curse you to your face![23]

In a matter of days Job had lost all his ten children, his business and his health. The devil's prediction was wrong—Job did not curse God.

The devil may be the enemy of the Father, but *the Father has deposed him*. We read: 'God did not spare the angels who sinned, but cast them down to hell and delivered them into chains of darkness to be reserved for judgment'.[24] God can only ever do one thing with sin or the source of sin—that is, to remove it from his presence. In deposing the devil the Father has cut off and cast from him the offending angels for ever.

The devil—the enemy of the Son

It had long been in the plan of God that he should send his dear Son to accomplish the work of dying to redeem mankind.[25] Employing a four-point strategy, the devil did his utmost to keep Christ from coming to the earth and carrying out his purpose.

To prevent Christ coming to earth

When Egypt was on the crest of a wave it had the whole nation of Israel as slaves building and working for them. Suddenly without provocation the king of Egypt spoke to the midwives and said: 'When you do the duties of a midwife for the Hebrew women . . . if it is a son, then you shall kill him.'[26] This was economic suicide and completely irrational. The intention was clear; to exterminate the Israelite nation for ever. If that had been done Christ could not have come to the earth.

The devil's intended destruction of Israel happened a second time. In about 475 BC the Persian king Ahasuerus (or Xerxes) reigned over 127 provinces from India to Ethiopia. Haman, the king's right-hand man, approached Ahasuerus and said: 'There is a certain people scattered and dispersed among the people in all the provinces of your kingdom.... If it pleases the king, let a decree be written that they be destroyed.' Permission was given: 'The money and the people are given to you, to do with them as seems good to you.'[27]

Both times the plots were thwarted. Both times the ancestral line, which was to lead to Jesus' birth, was protected. The devil's scheme was hindered.

To prevent Christ living on earth

Shortly after the birth of Jesus in Bethlehem, wise men came from the east asking Herod as to the whereabouts of a baby born to be king. In his anger Herod ordered the death of all baby boys under the age of two in Bethlehem.[28] The intention again was to prevent Christ from redeeming and reigning. Once more the devil was defeated and Christ lived.

Repeatedly throughout the life of Jesus, Satan sought to kill him and stirred up the minds and motives of evil men. When Christ read the Scriptures in the synagogue in Nazareth, the locals rose up in arms against him, and would have pushed him off a cliff if Jesus had not passed through their midst.[29] When Jesus was explaining his deity—that he was Jehovah, God in the flesh—the Jews were so angry they picked up stones to stone him to death, but Christ hid and escaped through the temple.[30] Even the winds and waves seemed to be under the control of the devil when Christ was asleep in a boat on the sea of Galilee. Experienced fishermen feared that they would perish in the water and so awoke Christ in panic. Christ stilled the storm and thus again the devil's intention to destroy him came to nothing.[31]

To prevent Christ living sinlessly on earth

At the start of his three-year ministry, Jesus was baptised and then went into the wilderness for forty days. He prayed, fasted, meditated on the Scriptures and was tempted. The devil appealed to Jesus physically, suggesting to him, when he had not eaten for forty days, to 'turn these stones into bread'. Afterwards the devil tempted the soul of Christ, saying 'cast yourself down from the temple', so that Christ would receive immediate acclaim and glory; later Satan attacked Jesus spiritually saying, in effect, I'll give you authority over this world right now, if you will 'bow down and worship me'. The devil tempted Christ in different places—first in the wilderness (symbolising the place of difficulty and discipline), secondly in the holy city (symbolising the place of duty, both secular and spiritual), and thirdly, on a high mountain (symbolising the place of devotion).[32] If Christ had fallen to any of these repeated temptations, his ministry would have been useless. If Christ had not been sinless, he could not have died paying for the sin of the world. Christ was the only individual whom the devil could not trap into sin.

Satan dogged the footsteps of Christ throughout the three years of ministry. Judas Iscariot, one of the twelve disciples, was referred to by Christ as 'a devil'.[33] Yet nothing the devil did could make Jesus sin.

To prevent Christ atoning for sin

How much the devil knew of or understood the plan of God in sending Christ to eventually die to pay for the world's sin, we do not know. However, it does seem as though the devil put it into the minds of those who gathered round the cross of Christ to shout up to him, 'He saved others; himself he cannot save. If he is the King of Israel, let him now come down from the cross, and we will believe him.'[34] Did the thought pass through his mind, 'They will believe me if I come down'? Certainly the devil subtly sought to spoil the great work of Christ. Jesus did save others, and to be able to save us, he knew that he must not save himself.

The devil utterly failed in preventing Christ coming to this earth and atoning for sin.

Jesus finished the work he had come to do. A way for forgiveness of sin has been made. Christ can bring us to God. But more has been achieved.

The enemy of Christ has been destroyed. The Father deposed the devil, but *Jesus has destroyed his work* and ultimately Satan himself:

> For this purpose the Son of God was manifested, that he might destroy the works of the devil.[35]

> Inasmuch then as the children have partaken of flesh and blood, he himself likewise shared in the same, that through death he might destroy him who had the power of death, that is, the devil.[36]

Warren Wiersbe in his Bible commentary[37] says:

> Destroy does not mean 'annihilate'. Satan is certainly still at work today! 'Destroy' here, means 'to render inoperative, to rob of power'. Satan has not been annihilated, but his power has been reduced and his weapons have been impaired. He is still a mighty foe, but he is no match for the power of God.

At the cost of his own life blood, Christ has taken the weapons of sin and death from the hand of the devil and thrust them into his heart, destroying his power for ever.

The devil—the enemy of the Holy Spirit

The Holy Spirit is God himself, at work in today's world. Jesus said of the Spirit:

> And when he has come, he will convict the world of sin, and of righteousness, and of judgment: of sin, because they do not believe in me; of righteousness, because I go to my

Father and you see me no more; of judgment, because the ruler of this world is judged.[38]

If you have ever been driving and looked in your mirror to see the flashing blue lights of a police car beckoning you to pull over, you will know how rapidly thoughts of self-examination flash through your mind— 'Is my indicator working...? Are my tyres all right...? Was I speeding...?' When God begins to work in a life he convicts a person in a similar way. Suddenly he becomes intensely aware of his own sin. Whereas previously he had thought himself to be all right, he becomes conscious of deep sinfulness. Like a plague or a cancer within, sin seems to have permeated all parts of his being. Nothing anyone says comforts him. It is the beginning of a period similar to gestation. God uses it to drive that person, whom he loves, to Christ.

However, the devil, the enemy of the Holy Spirit, puts a host of excuses into the mind of the sinner. It is as if Satan whispers, 'You can't help it...It's your upbringing...It's just the way you are...Everyone else does it...It's not sin but sickness.' There is no doubt that many factors such as family, environment, education and personality affect our actions and attitudes. However, the Bible clearly teaches that 'all have sinned and fall short of the glory of God'.[39] An early nineteenth century preacher, Robert Murray McCheyne expressed this same thought when he said in a sermon:

> When he has cast light into the sinner's bosom and let him see how every action of his life condemns him, and how vain it is to seek for any righteousness there, he then casts light upon the risen Saviour and says 'Look here'.

The Holy Spirit does not leave a person merely conscious of his own guilt before God; he then points the person's attention to Christ. He was righteous and altogether pure and holy. It was he who took the brunt of the weight of the world's wrongdoing on himself on the cross. He died taking the judgement of God against sin. The person who believes on Christ is not condemned and eternal life is guaranteed in God's word: see, for example, John 3:16,17 and John 5:24. Again, the argument of the devil is to counter this, arguing that Christ was merely a great religious leader who came to an unfortunate end. A mere cursory glance at the life of Christ will quickly reveal how untrue this notion is. Jesus himself said, 'The Son of Man is about to be betrayed into the hands of men, and they will kill him, and the third day he will be raised up';[40] and, 'The Son of Man [came] to give his life a ransom for many.'[41]

The devil is the enemy of the work of the Holy Spirit who seeks to take the gaze of people from themselves to Christ himself.[42] However, *the Holy Spirit defeats the devil.*

As soon as a person trusts the finished work of Jesus and receives forgiveness, God works a miracle in him; he is transformed within. Jesus called Christian conversion being 'born again';[43] Paul described it as being a 'new creation'.[44]

At conversion, the Holy Spirit completely changes individuals...

from having spiritual death to having spiritual life,[45]
from darkness to light,[46] and
from debt to liberty.[47]

Broken families and marred relationships have been mended as God, by his Holy Spirit, takes over a situation to defeat the devil and glorify Jesus Christ. Of course, a Christian is still under the attack of Satan. The Christian life is a spiritual warfare, but God gives Christ's strength to all who belong to him to be able to withstand the devil's pressures.

The devil—the enemy of us

As well as being the enemy of God, the devil also hates all human beings. Each was made in the image of God, no matter how marred they are now. God loves us and longs for our trust. The devil seeks to impair all that is of God in each person. Hell was made for the devil and his angels, but Satan will do all in his power to drag us down there too.

The Bible outlines three things which we are to do to overcome the devil:

Repent

To repent is to leave all known sin. It is not so much an act of the emotions, but of the will. It is taking God's side against our sin. Specifically, it means that the drunkard, relying on God's strength, will live soberly; the thief, honestly; the immoral person, purely; the gossip will speak kindly; the godless will live godly lives in Christ Jesus.

The great pattern-saint, Paul, in his missionary travels visited Ephesus. A great work of Christian conversion was done. Demonstrating their genuine repentance we read of the Ephesian Christians that 'many of those who had practised magic brought their books together and burned them in the sight of all. And they counted up the value of them, and it totalled fifty thousand pieces of silver.'[48]

Turning one's back on sin and the devil is a deliberate act of renouncing all the hidden works of darkness. It will mean burning books to do with the supernatural, destroying records whose symbols and themes are taken up with the devil, superstition, the occult or hell, and games that create interest in the occult.

Receive Christ

Having turned from sin, don't leave a vacuum; turn then to Christ. Jesus warned against merely making moral adjustments without true repentance and genuine faith:

> When an unclean spirit goes out of a man, he goes through dry places, seeking rest; and finding none, he says, 'I will return to my house from which I came.' And when he comes, he finds it swept and put in order. Then he goes and takes with him seven other spirits more wicked than himself, and they enter and dwell there; and the last state of that man is worse than the first.[49]

To be absolutely safe and secure from Satan's power, one needs not only to be emptied of self, but also filled with God himself. To receive Christ is to ask the one who died and rose from the dead to live within you as your forgiving Saviour and living Lord. The Bible teaches: 'But as many as received him, to them he gave the right to become children of God, even to those who believe in his name.'[50]

Resist the devil

Having repented of sin and received Christ, the Christian life is one of joyously walking with Christ. This involves a daily refusal of sin and resisting of Satan.

God promises that if we submit ourselves to him we can 'Resist the devil and he will flee from [us]'[51] and challenges us, 'nor give place to the devil'.[52]

Those who are prepared to take up the challenge, to trust and live for the God who made, died for, and calls them will be few. In the book of Revelation[53] we read that the devil deceives the whole world and all those who dwell on earth. Nevertheless Christ has promised his presence with those who will trust him: for he has said, 'I will never leave you nor forsake you.'[54]

A Royal Marine Commando professed Christian conversion through the work of a missioner in the Royal

Sailors' Rest in Singapore. Sadly though, he made no effort to change his lifestyle and showed no signs of spiritual progress. He inevitably went back to godless living. Eventually his ship was to sail on so the sailor went to the missioner to bid him farewell. The missioner said, 'I feel sorry for you.'

Amused, the sailor retorted, 'Why?'

The missioner took the sailor by the nose and pulled his head first in one direction and then another. 'I'll tell you why,' said the missioner. 'The devil has got you by the nose and is dragging you in any direction he wishes. The trouble is, you love it.'

The Bible described people being taken captive by the devil, at his will.[55] We need to realise that sin is attractive, especially in its early stages. The challenge is ours: will we follow the devil to hell or Christ to heaven? Do we belong to the kingdom of God or of Satan? Nobody can sit on the fence. There is no 'demilitarised zone' here!

Notes

1. Colossians 2:15.
2. James 4:7; 2 Corinthians 10:3–5; Ephesians 6:10–18.
3. 1 Samuel 28:8.
4. 1 Samuel 28:15.
5. Isaiah 8:19.
6. *Talk of the Devil* (Henry Walter Ltd, 1979, pp.35,36).
7. *Marx, Prophet of Darkness: Communism's Hidden Forces Revealed* (Marshall Pickering, 1986).
8. 1 Timothy 4:1.
9. 1 Corinthians 10:10; John 10:10.
10. Revelation 12:9.
11. John 8:44.
12. John 8:44.
13. Ephesians 2:2.
14. Genesis 3:1; Revelation 12:9.
15. 1 Peter 5:8.
16. 2 Corinthians 4:4.

17. John 10:10.
18. 2 Corinthians 12:7.
19. 1 Thessalonians 2:18.
20. Matthew 12:39; 16:3,4; 24:24; Mark 8:12; 13:22; Luke 11:29,30; John 4:48.
21. Quoted by Billy Graham, *Peace with God* (Word Books and STL Books, revised edn 1984, p.60).
22. Isaiah 14:12–15.
23. Job 1:9–11.
24. 2 Peter 2:4.
25. Revelation 13:8.
26. Exodus 1:16.
27. Esther 3:8–11.
28. Matthew 2:16–18.
29. Luke 4:28–31.
30. John 8:58,59.
31. Mark 4:35–41.
32. Matthew 4:1–11; Luke 4:1–13.
33. John 6:70,71.
34. Matthew 27:42.
35. 1 John 3:8.
36. Hebrews 2:14.
37. *The Bible Exposition Commentary,* Vol. 2 (Victor Books, 1989, p.506).
38. John 16:8–11.
39. Romans 3:23.
40. Matthew 17:22,23; see also 20:18,19.
41. Matthew 20:28.
42. John 16:13,14.
43. John 3:3.
44. 2 Corinthians 5:17.
45. Romans 6:23.
46. John 8:12.
47. John 8:32.
48. Acts 19:19.
49. Luke 11:24–26.
50. John 1:12.
51. James 4:7.
52. Ephesians 4:27.
53. Revelation 12:9; 13:14.
54. Hebrews 13:5.
55. 2 Timothy 2:26.

3

Why Believe the World Is Alienated From God?

For the creation was subjected to futility . . . the creation itself also will be delivered from the bondage of corruption into the glorious liberty of the children of God.
Romans 8:20,21

When Sir Winston Churchill wrote his autobiographical volume, *My Early Life*, he was able to satisfactorily fill in the details. When he penned his *History of the English Speaking Peoples*, it would remain incomplete. He could review the past and describe the present, but only God has a total view of the world. Past, present and future are all one in the eyes of the never-changing, timeless God.

His estimate of the world is comprehensive, unbiased and reliable. In contrast, ours is narrow, biased and often prejudiced. God knows tomorrow as yesterday and today in total. So what is his view of the place that is our temporary home? How does God see the world? In the Bible, what do we read of planet earth?

1. We discover that the world was wrought by God

In opening the Bible, on the very first page we read, 'In the beginning God created the heavens and the earth.'[1] The Psalms say, 'The earth is the Lord's and all its fullness, the world and those who dwell therein. For he has founded it upon the seas, and established it upon the waters.'[2] God is the Creator and rightful owner of all his creation. Just as footprints convinced Robinson Crusoe of the existence of another human being on his island, so too there are imprints of the Creator over all creation— God is seen everywhere in the world.

An idealist in the French Revolution arrogantly said to a believer, 'We intend to tear down every memory of the idea of God.' Quietly, the Christian replied, 'How will you get down the stars?'

The work of creation is awesome; therefore it is realistic to believe that God created it. Many dismiss Christianity and creation in the same way that the child looked up at the giraffe. It was the first time he had visited a zoo, and as he gazed at the long-legged, long-necked animal, he exclaimed, 'Ah, there's no such beast!' He had met something beyond his comprehension and outside his experience, so he concluded it could not be true. In contrast, read the words of King David in Psalm 8, written as he mused upon the wonder of creation.

O Lord, our Lord,
How excellent is your name in all the earth,
You who set your glory above the heavens!...
When I consider your heavens, the work of your fingers,
The moon and the stars, which you have ordained,
What is man that you are mindful of him,
And the son of man that you visit him?
For you have made him a little lower than the angels,
And you have crowned him with glory and honour.
You have made him to have dominion over the works of
    your hands;
You have put all things under his feet,
All sheep and oxen—
Even the beasts of the field,
The birds of the air,
And the fish of the sea
That pass through the paths of the seas.

O Lord, our Lord,
How excellent is your name in all the earth!

2. The world has been ruined by sin

The world which was created without flaw or fault, which was beautiful, perfect and sinless, experienced a moment of time when goodness and godliness were lost. There was an act of deliberate rebellion, when instead of becoming like God as had been promised to them by the serpent, Adam and Eve became like devils. The floodgate was opened. In rushed sin, suffering, sickness and death like an uncontrollable torrent, so that the world has never been the same since: 'through one man's offence judgment came to all men, resulting in condemnation';[3] 'the world through wisdom did not know God.'[4]

God has heard the cries both of the cynics and of the suffering: 'If there is a God why doesn't he stop the trouble?' or 'Why does he seem to stand so far away?' or 'Why does he appear to hide himself in times of suffering?'

Psalm 10 describes evil people. They have three basic mistaken views of God. They argue that he does not exist (verse 4) and so is false; then they say he does not see (verse 11) or has forgotten their wrong doing; and finally they believe that he does not judge (verse 13), but offers blanket forgiveness. People are often ready to admit that they are not as good as they ought to be, yet at the same time feel they do not deserve God's judgement.

On 7 December 1985 Police Constable William Clements gathered together his family for their daily Bible reading and prayer. Strangely, that day he read from Psalm 10, including the words found in verses 4 to 12:

The wicked in his proud countenance does not seek God;
God is in none of his thoughts.

His ways are always prospering;...
His mouth is full of cursing and deceit and oppression;
Under his tongue is trouble and iniquity.
He sits in the lurking places of the villages;
In the secret places he murders the innocent;
His eyes are secretly fixed on the helpless.
He lies in wait secretly, as a lion in his den;
He lies in wait to catch the poor;
He catches the poor when he draws him into his net.
So he crouches, he lies low,
That the helpless may fall by his strength.

In the afternoon he met another constable and together they went to the police station in Ballygawley, Co. Tyron, Northern Ireland, where they were based, to start their shift. Crouching in 'lurking places' of the villages were terrorist gunmen who shot William Clements and his colleague dead, and then blew up the police station. He was a victim of the type of person described in the psalm.

Jesus Christ himself fell prey to those who felt that God would not see their evil deeds.

Verse 14 of the psalm reassures its readers that God not only exists, but that he does see and will judge. However, at this present time we live in a world that, although made by God, is marred by man. Because of our sin, we have become enemies of the holy God.

The form of sin may change, but the fact of it does not. Humanism has sought to call sin sickness, and excuse it, blaming wrongdoing on education, environment or ecology, but God's absolute standard and basis of morality remain the same. Carl Meninger rightly asks through the title of his book, *Whatever Happened to Sin?*

God has given his unchanging law and uses it to make us aware of our true state. Two hundred words, engraved by the finger of God in tablets of stone, would condemn us all.

In Exodus chapter 20 we read the Ten Commandments:

And God spoke all these words, saying:...
You shall have no other gods before me.
You shall not make for yourself any carved image, or any
    likeness of anything that is in heaven above, or that is in
    the earth beneath, or that is in the water under the earth;
you shall not bow down to them nor serve them....
You shall not take the name of the Lord your God in
    vain....
Remember the Sabbath day, to keep it holy....
Honour your father and your mother, that your days may be
    long upon the land which the Lord your God is giving
    you.
You shall not murder.
You shall not commit adultery.
You shall not steal.
You shall not bear false witness against your neighbour.
You shall not covet....

In attitude and action we all fall short. Covering up with respectability, religion or self-righteousness does not change our true nature. 'Wash a pig as much as you like, but it goes right back to the mud' says the Russian proverb.

Over and again, the Bible describes the world as failing. In Galatians we read of this 'present evil age';[5] in Ephesians of 'the rulers of the darkness of this age';[6] in Corinthians it speaks of those 'whose minds the god of this age has blinded, who do not believe, lest the light of the gospel of the glory of Christ, who is the image of God, should shine on them.'[7]

No wonder one writer has described this world's system and scheming as 'rearranging the deck-chairs on the *Titanic* while it is sinking'.

As such, the picture painted is dark and dreary, but God has master-strokes that transform this whole view of the world.

3. The world has been reclaimed by Christ

In speaking to individuals, I often say, 'Christ Jesus came into the world to save sinners…and you and I qualify.' Rarely does anyone disagree with that. Instead of God, godliness and goodness, the world's trinity is pleasure, treasure and leisure.

Despite the mad race for these, rarely is the world content. It appears orphaned. William Haddad was an associate of the Kennedy's. After J.F. Kennedy was assassinated, his young son, John, asked Mr Haddad, 'Are you a daddy?' Haddad admitted that he was. Said little John, 'Then will you throw me up in the air?'[8]

Similarly, the world searches for a fullness and fulfilment it cannot find because the vital link we were made to have between God and ourselves has been severed by sin. 'But your iniquities have separated you from your God; and your sins have hidden his face from you.'[9]

Into this type of world Christ was born. He came to take away the sin of us all. He is called 'the Saviour of the world'.[10]

After living a life that was pure and holy, he engaged in mortal conflict with the world, sin, Satan, death and hell. In the hours of darkness hanging on the cross he, like the world when it rebelled against God, was stripped of his dignity and covered with sin. All that keeps a person from God and would condemn him to hell was laid on the Lord Jesus as he paid the price for the world's sin. God devised a means whereby we who are banished from him may be brought to God through the death of his Son.

The significance of the cross is that God was in Christ reconciling the world to himself. By raising him from the dead, God demonstrated to a watching and waiting world Christ's victory over sin and death.

4. The world will ultimately be restored and remade by God

God's plan for his creation is by no means over.

There have been many false prophecies. In 1901 Wilbur Wright predicted that there would be no powered flight for seventy years. Two years later, he was flying the skies! In the early 1970s, Margaret Thatcher said, 'There will not be a female prime minister in my life time!'

God, however, never makes false prophecies. He has a timetable for this world.

A little girl, returning home from school, stopped to listen to the market square clock chiming out the time. Something had evidently gone wrong, for it went on striking twelve, thirteen, fourteen, fifteen... She ran to her mother shouting, 'Mummy, it's later than it's ever been before!'

One day the world as we know it will cease. The apostle Peter wrote:

> The heavens will pass away with a great noise, and the elements will melt with fervent heat; both the earth and the works that are in it will be burned up.... Nevertheless we, according to his promise, look for new heavens and a new earth.'[11]

In this time, Christ will be acknowledged as the King of kings and Lord of lords, as he takes his rightful place on the throne governing this earth. This will be the world's greatest reclamation scheme. The history of the world will have gone full circle. It was wrought by God, ruined by sin, reclaimed by Christ, but will be restored and remade by God.

Interestingly, the history of the world is likewise the story of every true Christian.

1. Christians recognise that they are individually wrought by God

No birth is an 'accident'. God is in control even though circumstances may sometimes be sad. Each person has been fearfully and wonderfully made and God has a perfect plan for each. To perceive this immediately brings a sense of responsibility. Watch a commercial van driver tearing round corners, screeching to a halt and burning up the tyres as he sets off at a set of lights. He treats the vehicle badly because he does not own it. If, however, he buys even a second-hand car for himself, how carefully that prized possession is cleaned, polished, driven and serviced! A sense of owning or being owned affects our behaviour. The point is not so much a political one but a theological one.

An atheist does not feel accountable to anyone, and declares himself free of responsibility, but a believer is aware that there is someone whose watchful eye weighs all actions and activities.

2. Christians are keenly aware that they have been ruined by sin

In the book of Romans, the apostle Paul lists Old Testament quotes to illustrate the sinfulness of each person:

> There is none righteous, no, not one;
> There is none who understands;
> There is none who seeks after God.
> They have all gone out of the way;
> They have together become unprofitable;
> There is none who does good, no, not one.
> Their throat is an open tomb;
> With their tongues they have practised deceit;
> The poison of asps is under their lips;
> Whose mouth is full of cursing and bitterness.
> Their feet are swift to shed blood;
> Destruction and misery are in their ways;

And the way of peace they have not known.
There is no fear of God before their eyes.[12]

Professor Hallesby in his book *Religious or Christian?*
says:

Men fill the world with their sins. Sins of every kind and of
every degree: conscious sin and unconscious sin; individual
sin and social sin; national sin and international sin; open sin
and secret sin; sin that is afraid and conceals itself in dark
places, and bold sin, openly committed. But the worst thing
about man is not that he does that which is sinful. The
unregenerate heart of man is worse than all his sinful deeds.
'For from within, out of the heart of men, proceed evil
thoughts, adulteries, fornications, murders, thefts, covet-
ousness, wickedness, deceit, licentiousness, an evil eye,
blasphemy, pride, foolishness.'[13]

Christian hymn-writers have also expressed their con-
sciousness of wrongdoing. For example, in his famous
hymn *Rock of Ages* Toplady says:

Nothing in my hand I bring;
Simply to thy cross I cling;
Naked, come to thee for dress;
Helpless, look to thee for grace;
Foul, I to the fountain fly;
Wash me, Saviour, or I die.

So many feel that their good works will hopefully pave
a way to heaven, but even one sin, if not confessed
before the Lord and thereby forgiven and blotted out, is
serious enough to keep us from God eternally. On virtually the last page of the Bible, speaking of heaven, we
read, 'But there shall by no means enter it anything that
defiles, or causes an abomination or a lie.'[14]

Jesus met a man with a withered arm. Both were in
the synagogue, where religious folk would be looking
on. Jesus commanded, 'Stretch out your hand.' Which

hand was he speaking about? The answer appears obvious, namely the withered arm. Indeed that is the one that was outstretched and healed by the power of Christ. Most people, however, like to 'stretch out their good arm'. They speak of giving to charity, paying one hundred pence in the pound, of never doing anybody any harm, or of attending church. Christ is unwilling and unable to help such. He said that he came to seek and save those who are lost.[15] If we would 'stretch out our withered arm' and confess our sins, we would find that 'he is faithful and just to forgive us our sins and to cleanse us from all unrighteousness'.[16] A sick person, not someone who is well, goes to a doctor. In like manner, only those who recognise their need will feel they must 'go to' the Saviour. A respectable Yorkshire parish church caused a stir when outside they put a huge banner saying, 'Only sinners welcome here'. They were right!

3. The Christian has been reclaimed by Christ

True Christian experience begins when one enters into a living and personal relationship with God. Christ died to buy us or redeem us. Christians no longer belong to themselves. They have been bought with the price of the precious blood of Christ and therefore belong to him.[17]

Christian conversion is an act of God in the life of a person who, by an act of their mind and will, turn from their own life to serve the living and true God.[18] At this moment God turns to the individual to forgive the past and guide the future. God can do this on the basis of the finished work of Jesus Christ.

4. The Bible teaches that God restores and remakes those who believe on Christ

Jesus spoke of being 'born again' or 'born from above'.[19] Paul wrote, 'Therefore if anyone is in Christ, he is a new creation; old things have passed away; behold, all things have become new.'[20]

In the moment of Christian conversion, God by his Holy Spirit makes the new believer his dwelling place. As the years of Christian life begin to unfold, God refines the individual. Bad people are made good. Tempers are calmed, tongues are controlled, dishonesty and impurity are defeated, to be replaced by integrity and morality. Ultimately, on that final, resurrection day, the work of sin and death will be totally reversed.

Notes

1. Genesis 1:1.
2. Psalm 24:1.
3. Romans 5:18.
4. 1 Corinthians 1:21.
5. Galatians 1:4.
6. Ephesians 6:12.
7. 2 Corinthians 4:4.
8. Fadiman (ed.), *Faber Book of Anecdotes* (Faber & Faber, 1985).
9. Isaiah 59:2.
10. John 4:42; 1 John 4:14.
11. 2 Peter 3:10,13.
12. Romans 3:10–18.
13. Mark 7:21,22.
14. Revelation 21:27.
15. Luke 19:10.
16. 1 John 1:9.
17. 1 Peter 1:18,19; 1 Corinthians 6:19,20.
18. 1 Thessalonians 1:9.
19. John 3.
20. 2 Corinthians 5:17. See also chapter 5 of this book.

4

Why Believe Jesus Is the Son of God?

Peter said: *You are the Christ, the Son of the living God.*
Matthew 16:16

Jesus said: *I and my Father are one.*
John 10:30

The most influential man of all time was born and reared in obscurity. He has changed the lives of millions. He has turned upside down the culture of nations. He has altered the course of world history.

Jesus Christ is the theme of the world's best selling book, the Bible. Millions of other books and songs have been written about him. So who was Jesus of Nazareth? Christians believe he was more than mere mortal—he was 'God manifest in the flesh'.

Jesus Christ—a man

Jesus was conceived in the womb of a virgin. He was laid in a manger as a helpless baby. He grew to be a toddler, adolescent, young adult and mature man. He was subject to the authority of Mary and Joseph. He showed loyalty to the social and political conditions of the day.

Physically, Christ experienced hunger, thirst, weariness, pain and privation, yet exercised self-control, self-denial, humility, calmness, endurance and wisdom.

Emotionally, Jesus was no stranger to joy and sorrow, wonder and amazement, love and anger, indignation and compassion. He used humour, yet wept at the tomb of his friend Lazarus. He had an unswerving sense of duty and destiny.

Socially, Jesus was involved with the activities of people and society. He was invited to and attended the wedding feast at Cana in Galilee. He accepted invitations to meals. We read of his involvement in adult years with his mother, brothers and sisters. He had special friends and valued companionship. Even in his last moments on the cross, Christ made provision for his mother and beloved disciple John, giving each responsibility for the other. Jesus was distant and yet accessible.

Jesus was not the 'hippy' drop-out philosopher as he is sometimes portrayed. His thinking and teaching were intuitive, spiritual and practical. He was not an echo of other voices, but the original voice. His teaching was not abstract or negative, but concrete and positive.

No wonder that twenty centuries on from the completion of his life on earth, there is profound interest and fascination in his life and work. Even the greatest sceptic or openly blasphemous prove by continually speaking of him that he is a man they cannot leave alone.

Jesus Christ—a mighty man

On examination of the Gospels of Matthew, Mark, Luke and John, Christ is seen clearly portrayed as being more than 'head and shoulders' above other men.

Jesus never apologised—nor needed to! He did not blush with embarrassment or shame. He never had to withdraw a word. He showed no sign of regret or remorse. Jesus did not suffer the pain of an accusing conscience. In fact he was bold enough to ask his enemies, 'Which of you convicts me of sin?'[1] Not a question most of us would dare bandy about! Such was

the character and calibre of the life of Christ that even
men like Judas, who betrayed Christ for a mere thirty
pieces of silver, later committed suicide having cried, 'I
have sinned by betraying innocent blood.'[2] Pilate, who
sentenced Jesus to crucifixion, appealed to Christ's
accusers asking, 'Why, what evil has he done? I find no
fault in him.'[3] The Roman executioner said of him,
'Truly this was the Son of God!'[4]

The sinlessness of Jesus demonstrated itself in his
attitude to people. He loved his enemies; he was patient
with his friends; he met the needs of the crowds; he went
alongside outcasts; he delighted to do the will of his
Father in heaven; and he died willingly for you and me,
paying for our sin.

There were no character defects in Christ. He was not
only without sin, but without weakness also. There was
an equilibrium and balance of personality in Christ. He
demonstrated great haste and energy, but he also knew
how to rest and be still. He could be very severe but
deeply tender and compassionate. He was a man of great
dignity and stature but humbled himself to wash the feet
of his disciples (including Judas), and eventually even to
death on the cross. While needing times of solitude, he
was yet sociable; solemn but joyful, and greatly profound but pleasingly straightforward.

Jesus Christ—more than a man

To be true to the Bible's teaching about Jesus Christ is to
accept humbly that your mind or intellect is unable to
understand all things. Some things are beyond human
comprehension. No-one can ever fully comprehend the
God who has revealed himself as infinite, inexhaustible
and eternal.

However, the Bible clearly teaches that God became
a man. Deity became dust. God clothed himself in a
human body. He was encased in flesh. God was big

enough to become small, strong enough to become weak—as small and weak as a tiny foetus in a mother's womb, later to be a little baby wrapped in swaddling clothes and laid in a manger. This was the mighty maker of all becoming like the people he had made—the Creator becoming as one of his creatures.

In a school nativity play, a little boy appeared as the third wise man. However, when he came on stage he saw his mother and father sitting in the audience and was utterly awestruck. His lines went as his mind went completely blank.

Eventually, he knelt down to present the myrrh to 'baby Jesus' in the manger. He just could not remember what to say. After an embarrassing silence the exasperated teacher whispered, 'Say something!' Instead, silence still reigned.

'Say anything,' called the teacher in desperation.

Suddenly the boy blurted out, 'Ay, he's just like his dad!'

The Creator God did come to earth, and he was 'just like' his Father. He was destined by God to go to the cross, to redeem this lost world. Rising again, he was to ascend to heaven.

Colonel James Irwin of the Apollo XV Mission was right when he said, 'God walking on earth is more important than man walking on the moon.'

Let me give four proofs that Jesus is himself God.

1. He is called what only God is called

Both the Old and New Testaments speak of Christ's deity. Repeatedly in the Old Testament Messiah's coming and work are prophesied. Handel's *Messiah* takes up the words of Isaiah written about 700 BC:

For unto us a Child is born, unto us a Son is given; and the government will be upon his shoulder. And his name will be

called Wonderful, Counsellor, Mighty God, Everlasting
Father, Prince of Peace.[5]

Micah writing about 710 BC said:

But you, Bethlehem Ephrathah, though you are little
among the thousands of Judah, yet out of you shall come
forth to me the one to be ruler in Israel, whose goings forth
have been from of old, from everlasting.[6]

In the Old Testament there are over seven thousand
references to the sacred name of God, usually rendered
Yahweh or Jehovah. In the New Testament, his name is
rendered Lord. This exalted title is applied directly to
Jesus.[7] Clearly Jesus is Jehovah. In fact, the Lord Jesus
took God's own title to refer to himself, calling himself
the 'I AM'.[8]

Over forty times, New Testament writers call Christ
the 'Son of God'. This name is associated with Jesus in
his baptism,[9] in his temptations,[10] his miracles[11] and his
sufferings.[12]

Five times Jesus is called 'the only begotten Son of
God'. The word 'begotten' is an important one: 'It indi-
cates that, as the Son of God, he was the sole represent-
ative of the being and character of the one who sent
him.'[13]

Christ is called the Alpha and Omega, the first and the
last.[14] Repeatedly, the New Testament in such very clear
terms calls Christ God. For example:

In the beginning was the Word, and the Word was with
God, and the Word was God.... And the Word became
flesh and dwelt among us.[15]

No one has seen God at any time. The only begotten Son,
who is in the bosom of the Father, he has declared him.[16]

And Thomas answered, and said to him, 'My Lord and my
God!'[17]

The church of God which he purchased with his own blood.[18]

But to the Son he says: 'Your throne, O God, is for ever and ever.'[19]

Christ came, who is over all, the eternally blessed God. Amen.[20]

'Behold, a virgin shall be with child, and bear a Son, and they shall call his name Immanuel,' which is translated, 'God with us.'[21]

Looking for the blessed hope and glorious appearing of our great God and Saviour Jesus Christ.[22]

Even Jesus' preferred self-designation 'Son of Man' often carries great significance. The title comes from the Old Testament[23] where the Son of Man, who is a heavenly figure, appears at the close of history as the judge, lord and heir of all the kingdoms of the world. It is a title particularly bound up with the idea of judgement, which is a role reserved exclusively for God.

Very plainly Jesus is called what only God is called.

2. He is like what only God is like

Too often people create their own image of God. One hears statements such as, 'My view of God is...' Frankly, an individual caricature of God is of little importance. What is vital is God's revelation of his own character. The Bible is that revelation.

It describes four basic attributes of God: his omnipotence (total power), his omniscience (total knowledge), his omnipresence total presence), and his immutability (total changelessness). We also read that he is eternal, sinless, just, loving, holy and consistent.

The Bible reveals God as a Trinity. He is one God in

three distinguishable persons. Human thought and language are strained to try and grasp or explain this infinite truth. God would not be God and humans would not be human if we could truly comprehend him. Each person of the Godhead is divine: the Father is God[24]; the Son is God[25]; and the Holy Spirit is God.[26] As the hymn expresses it:

> Holy, holy, holy! Merciful and mighty!
> God in three persons, blessed Trinity!

Jesus' deity can be seen in that his attributes are indeed uniquely God's. Yet since he was God confined by the human body in which he was 'dressed', there were clearly self-imposed limitations on these attributes.

Although chosing to lay aside the omnipotence that was his in heaven, Jesus nevertheless often demonstrated his power. On one occasion he was asleep in the stern of a boat on the Sea of Galilee. A severe storm suddenly arose; the disciples, in a state of panic, awakened him crying, 'Teacher, do you not care that we are perishing?' Jesus immediately stilled the storm with the words, 'Peace, be still.' The wind ceased and there was a great calm. Understandably the disciples said one to another, 'Who can this be, that even the wind and the sea obey him!'[27] With this same power, Christ fed over five thousand with a mere five loaves and two fishes. He cured the lame and leprous, the blind, deaf and dumb, the paralysed and palsied. He cast out demons and even raised the dead. Then, after the resurrection, God restored to Christ all authority in heaven and on earth and exalted him, seating him at his right hand in the heavenly places (read Matthew 28:18, Ephesians 1:19–23 and Philippians 2:8–11). He is truly omnipotent.

In Luke's Gospel, chapter 2 verses 41 to 52, we see Jesus learning and listening. We read of him at the age of twelve sitting in the midst of the doctors of the law talking and asking questions. However, even at such a young age he left these learned men astonished at his understanding and answers. After this he continued to increase in wisdom and stature. It was the same Jesus who was later to show that he knew the thoughts and secret whisperings of both the disciples and those who plotted against him, by revealing their thoughts. Today he is the one from whom nothing is hidden; he knows the details of all our lives. Christ is omniscient.

Once again, we see God who is omnipresent, confined to human form in Jesus Christ. During his earthly ministry Christ was in only one place at a time. However, looking forward to a time after his resurrection, Jesus made promises such as: 'For where two or three are gathered together in my name, I am there in the midst of them'[28] and 'lo, I am with you always, even to the end of the age.'[29] These assurances establish Christ's omnipresence.

As far as Christ's unchanging nature is concerned, we read:

And he is before all things and in him all things consist.[30]

But you are the same, and your years will not fail.[31]

Jesus Christ is the same yesterday, today, and for ever.[32]

As Christ revealed his divine attributes to his disciples, so they realised their own sinfulness. When Peter saw Christ's omniscience, he cried, 'Depart from me, for I am a sinful man, O Lord!'[33]

What it must have been for the disciples to spend their years with Christ who is described as 'holy, harmless, undefiled, separate from sinners'![34] They bickered and quarrelled; he did not. They showed pride and selfishness; he would not. They sinned; he could not.

John, who was especially close, said, 'In him is no sin'; Paul the great thinker said, 'He knew no sin'; Peter the man of action said, 'He did no sin'; and the book of Hebrews sums it up with the categorical 'He is without sin'. Only God is so pure and holy.

Then again we see Christ demonstrating God's love and justice throughout his life in all his dealings with people. Different needs were met. His love was never at the expense of justice nor his justice devoid of love. Love and justice met at the cross. Apparently opposing forces married together perfectly when Jesus died. It was infinite love for rebel sinners, such as we all are, that took Christ to Calvary where he would hang naked. Neither Roman soldiers nor nails held Jesus to the cross, but *love*. The arms of Christ were outstretched as if to go to every 'nook and cranny' of every human heart to draw to himself the sin of all. God's righteous justice judged the sin of all by actually punishing Christ, the substitute, so as to be able to forgive us, the sinners. 'For Christ also suffered once for sins, the just for the unjust, that he might bring us to God.'[35]

3. He acts as only God acts

God is an active God. Labour and work are intrinsically bound up in the nature of God (and incidentally, in those who would follow him).

The work of Christ was such that it can only be explained as being divine. This is seen in four ways.

His creation

In every great act of God the Trinity is at work. We read in Genesis that God said, 'Let us make man in our image, according to our likeness.'[36] The plurality of the personality of God is seen in this verse. God spoke, the Spirit hovered over the face of the waters, but, 'All things were made through him [Christ], and without him nothing was made that was made.'[37]

Later in the Bible the apostle Paul wrote:

He is the image of the invisible God, the firstborn over all creation. For by him all things were created that are in heaven and that are on earth, visible and invisible, whether thrones or dominions or principalities or powers. All things were created through him and for him.[38]

If God is the Creator, and the Creator is Christ, then Christ is God!

His teaching

People say, 'Practise what you preach': Jesus preached what he practised. His life and teachings were utterly consistent. His words were original, straightforward, profound, picturesque, concrete, practical, brief and authoritative. He rarely quoted others, but no-one has been so often quoted. He never wrote a book, but libraries are 'full of' writings concerning him. He spoke and others silently listened. Nothing he said has had to be corrected with the passage of time, but the world is still to see one person who will fully obey his teaching. Religious officers, who were sent by the Pharisees and chief priests to trap him, came back and reported, 'No man ever spoke like this man.' They were more right than they imagined! No wonder the common people heard him gladly.

His miracles

The miracles of Christ can only be explained by the power of God at work. C.S. Lewis has argued:

The miracles...are a retelling in small letters of the very same story which is written across the whole world in letters too large for some of us to see....In other words, some of the miracles do locally what God has already done universally: others do locally what he has not yet done, but will do.[39]

For example, when Christ turned water into wine at

Cana in Galilee, he was taking off the mask. Each year God turns water into wine. He creates the vine and teaches it to draw up water by its roots and, with the sun's help, to turn that water into a juice that will ferment and take on certain qualities. We call it a law of nature. Christ's miracle was simply short-cutting the process.

Or again, year by year God turns a little corn into much corn—the seed is sown and there is an increase. Similarly, in every bay and river the slow process of the multiplication of fish is constantly at work. However, when Jesus fed both the five thousand and the four thousand he short-circuited this process. A little bread and a few fish were miraculously multiplied to feed the crowds. Christ's work was God's work with the mask off.

The miracles of healing fall into the same pattern. The work of healing is not so much in the medicine but the patient's body (it would be no use bandaging a dead body, there must be life for there to be recovery). Christ cured people visibly and instantly, again cutting short the inward process with which we are more familiar.

Jesus, the Son of God, only does what he sees the Father do.[40] As C.S. Lewis puts it, 'There is, so to speak, a family style.'[41] Christ's miraculous work is evidence of his deity. He was doing the work of God.

His death

Death and mortality have no part in the existence and being of God, the immortal and eternal God. Death came into this world as a result of sin. God had warned Adam, 'but from the tree of the knowledge of good and evil you shall not eat, for in the day that you eat of it you shall surely die.'[42]

Jesus never sinned and therefore death could not touch him. He could say to a group who were his enemies, 'No one takes it [his life] from me, but I lay it down of myself. I have power to lay it down, and I have power to take it again.'[43]

Yet strangely, Christ was the only man born to die. In fact he was the only one who chose to die (in contrast to a person who commits suicide, who merely decides when he dies, not whether he dies). However, when Christ was crucified he was fulfilling the eternal plan of heaven to save men and women, the Old Testament pictures and prophecies, and his own aim and purpose.

Jesus was not just a martyr or example. His death was not merely a quirk of history but rather a part of God's greatest act. Hanging on the cross in agony, humiliation and shame, God transferred the sin of the world on to Christ.

God took the sins of wrong attitudes and actions; sins of the past, present and future; the sins we have forgotten and those we wish we could forget; the wrong we regret and that which we revel in; then laid it all upon Christ. The sins of millions were put on him. Such a crushing load contracted and compacted into three hours would have killed any other instantly. However, Christ—God in human form—carried them all. They never polluted his heart but he bore them all. He was actually made sin for us.[44]

To carry such a load, to be able to atone for that weight of sin, to be able to pay the eternal punishment in three hours of agony and trauma, is sufficient evidence that Jesus is himself God. 'God was in Christ reconciling the world to himself.'[45]

His resurrection

Throughout the ages the names of conquerors have come and gone—Alexander, Julius Caesar, Napoleon, Hitler. One conqueror has, however, defeated them all. That is the conqueror 'death'. Herod killed the baby boys in Bethlehem, Nero the Christians in Rome, Hitler the Jews and Stalin his political opponents; but the conqueror 'death' has been totally indiscriminate. All have been overpowered by him—except one.

Christ died, was buried and rose from the dead. No other religious founder or leader has ever done that.

The historical evidence for this great event is absolutely watertight. Jesus himself had prophesied it: 'Destroy this temple, and in three days I will raise it up....But he was speaking of the temple of his body.'[46] The disciples and others were witnesses to it. Christ's opponents could not explain it and hundreds of early Christians experienced it!

This is not a cunningly devised fable, nor Christian mythology, but established fact. Let us note that:

(a) *There is no doubt that he was dead.* Before the crucifixion the back of Jesus had been beaten with many lashes. They had buffeted him, spat on him and wedged a crown of thorns on his head. He was made to carry on his torn back a rough, rugged Roman cross. Nailed through his hands and feet, he was suspended up on the wooden beams. He drank nothing to alleviate the pain. Over and above the physical and emotional hurt was the spiritual suffering. Christ, the sinless one, took the sin of the world on himself. After fully paying the price of all sin he victoriously cried out, 'It is finished!' and voluntarily 'gave up his spirit' as John's Gospel records in chapter 19, verse 30.

Professional executioners, as the Roman guards were, saw that he was dead but just to make sure, they thrust a spear into his side. Blood and water poured out, showing that there had been certain death.

(b) *There was no opportunity for the body to be stolen.* Christ's corpse was laid in the tomb in the evening before sunset. Cloth was wrapped around his body and head separately.[47]

A huge stone was rolled in front of the tomb and a guard placed around it lest his body be stolen. The soldiers would be under threat of death if the body disappeared. On the third day, on the first Easter Sunday morning, the stone had been rolled away to reveal that, though the clothing was left intact, the body of Jesus had gone—HE HAD RISEN.

(c) There is no possibility of it being a lie. During the next forty days Christ appeared to various groups of people[48] including: two women; two men walking to Emmaus; two, then ten, then the eleven disciples; and also to a group of over five hundred people at one time.

These resurrection appearances were such that the antagonistic authorities were unable to dispute them. They were in different circumstances at different times in varying places. Neither Romans nor Jews, who would have loved to have disproved the resurrection of Jesus by producing his dead body, were able to refute the facts: the tomb was empty, with the body not only gone but the living Jesus appearing to many. Most of the disciples were to seal with their blood their testimony that they had seen the risen Christ alive. Would they do this for a lie?

(d) There is no explanation except that Christ rose from the dead. It was a clear resurrection—not mystical or spiritual, but physical. To the disciples Jesus said: 'Behold my hands and my feet, that it is I myself. Handle me and see, for a spirit does not have flesh and bones as you see I have.'[49]

Thomas's reaction to the risen Christ is the only sufficiently expressive one: 'My Lord and my God!'[50]

In the forty days after the resurrection Christ appeared to complete his teaching of the disciples and bring them to a confident assurance of his defeat of death and his eventual return to establish fully his kingdom on earth.

It was a climactic appearance that brought Christ's work to a completion. This happened when a cloud manifesting God's presence and glory took away Jesus.

This, plus his present exaltation and his promised return,[51] are confirmation of the deity of Christ who shares in the glory of God and will one day reign on earth.

4. He claims what only God claims

If you were God, how would you get the attention of the world; by a lightning bolt or a message in the sky?

So often God's method is to send a baby. When he was to deliver the people of Israel from Egypt, God sent the baby Moses; when he was to judge Israel righteously he sent a baby—Samuel; when he was to prepare the way for the coming of Christ, God sent the baby John; and when the Saviour of the world was to come, he came in the form of a baby.

Whereas others have pointed the way to God, Jesus pointed to himself as the way: 'And he said to them, "Follow me, and I will make you fishers of men"'[52] or, 'Come to me, all you who labour and are heavy laden, and I will give you rest.'[53] This was not vain arrogance or megalomania. He is the unique way to God. 'I am the way, the truth, and the life. No one comes to the Father except through me.'[54]

If Jesus were not God this would have been pure presumption, but millions have proved the truth of his claims.

He claimed to be the life-giver. He said, 'And I give them eternal life, and they shall never perish; neither shall anyone snatch them out of my hand.'[55] Only God can give life.

Christ promised a truly satisfying life: 'but whoever drinks of the water that I shall give him will never thirst. But the water that I shall give him will become in him a fountain of water springing up into everlasting life.'[56] Only God is not a disappointment, offering such life.

Christ pre-eminently claims to be able to forgive sin.

On one occasion[57] Jesus said to a paralytic, 'Your sins are forgiven you.' Some scribes immediately questioned this reasoning, saying that Christ was speaking blasphemously because only God can forgive sins.

Christ is God and because of his death and resurrection offers to all who will trust him forgiveness and new life. This is an offer only God can make.

Jesus, the God-man, deserves to be the God of your life.

Notes

1. John 8:46.
2. Matthew 27:4.
3. Luke 23:22.
4. Matthew 27:54.
5. Isaiah 9:6.
6. Micah 5:2.
7. 1 Peter 3:22 applies Psalm 110:1; Romans 10:13 applies Joel 2:32; Philippians 2:9–11 applies Isaiah 45:23; see also John 12:41 and Ephesians 4:8 applies Psalm 68:18.
8. Exodus 3:14; cf. John 8:58; 6:35; 8:12,24; 10:7,11; 11:25; 14:6; 15:1; 18:5ff.; Mark 14:62.
9. Mark 1:11.
10. Matthew 4:3,6.
11. John 9:35.
12. Matthew 16:16,21; Mark 15:39.
13. *Vine's Expository Dictionary of New Testament Words*.
14. Revelation 1:8,17; 22:13.
15. John 1:1,14.
16. John 1:18.
17. John 20:28.
18. Acts 20:28.
19. Hebrews 1:8.
20. Romans 9:5.
21. Matthew 1:23.
22. Titus 2:13.
23. Daniel 7:13.
24. Matthew 6:8ff.; 7:21; Galatians 1:1.

25. John 1:1,14,18; Romans 9:5; Colossians 2:9; Titus 2:13; Hebrews 1:8–10.
26. Mark 3:29; John 15:26; 1 Corinthians 6:19; 2 Corinthians 3:17ff.
27. Mark 4:35–41.
28. Matthew 18:20.
29. Matthew 28:20.
30. Colossians 1:17.
31. Hebrews 1:12.
32. Hebrews 13:8.
33. Luke 5:8.
34. Hebrews 7:26.
35. 1 Peter 3:18.
36. Genesis 1:26.
37. John 1:3.
38. Colossians 1:15,16.
39. *God in the Dock* (Fount Paperbacks, 1979).
40. John 5:19.
41. Ibid.
42. Genesis 2:17.
43. John 10:18.
44. 2 Corinthians 5:21.
45. 2 Corinthians 5:19.
46. John 2:19–21.
47. John 20:5–7.
48. Many are mentioned in 1 Corinthians chapter 15.
49. Luke 24:39.
50. John 20:28.
51. Acts 1:9–11.
52. Matthew 4:19.
53. Matthew 11:28.
54. John 14:6.
55. John 10:28.
56. John 4:14.
57. Mark 2:2–13.

5

Why Believe Death Has Been Defeated by God?

. . . that through death he might destroy him who had the power of death, that is, the devil, and release those who through fear of death were all their lifetime subject to bondage.
Hebrews 2:14,15

'I'm not afraid to die. I just don't want to be there when it happens.' Woody Allen's famous quote vocalises the silent fears of most people.

Sadly, we give our lives to learning to live, but before the lessons are fully learnt, life is taken from us.

Life is so short. The Bible likens it to a tale that is told; to a vapour, which is here one minute and gone the next; to a shadow; to the speed of a weaver's shuttle in a loom; to grass or flowers blooming for a few days but then being cut down and withering. There is a mark on every tombstone that is highly significant. Between the dates of birth and death is a hyphen. It is just a small dash. Such is life: a short span between birth and death.

Inevitably, there is grieving at the loss of a member of a family, when a friend is taken, or a colleague, or a neighbour.

Death is separation. Physical death is the severing of the link between the human spirit and body. 'Then the dust will return to the earth as it was, and the spirit will return to God who gave it.'[1]

However, death is far worse than merely an enemy wanting to conquer the body. It can take many forms.

There is *moral* death. For the promiscuous, learning the facts of life gives them the key to moral decay and death.

There is *intellectual* death. Rather than pursue a course of study, the 'drop-outs' opt out of society and end their intellectual pursuit.

There is *social* death. This is the result for hermits who isolate themselves from the fabric and friendship of society.

There is *spiritual* death. This is the result of sin and afflicts every human being until the human spirit is born again. Sin separates us from our Creator.

Fear of death holds captive those who will eventually and inevitably become its victims. Yet, the Christian gospel offers an answer to death. The conqueror has been conquered; the enemy has been defeated. This is nowhere better expressed than in Paul's letter to the Christians living in Corinth: 'The sting of death is sin, and the strength of sin is the law. But thanks be to God, who gives us the victory through our Lord Jesus Christ.'[2]

We will look at the teaching of this verse and see its most salient points and their relevance to us.

The grave

First, we see the grave—it is inevitable. The verse talks about 'the sting of death'. Nobody knows when he will die, though he knows he must. I have only met one person so utterly deceived that she really feels she will never die. The awful reality for her error will one day dawn on her. Obviously, we cannot go though life constantly thinking of the day of death, but we need to be sure that we are at least ready. I could not enjoy the journey if I felt that the end was to be a crash landing!

For eight years I worked with a Christian man who

died of cancer, aged forty-seven. Though an indefatigable lay preacher, his most powerful sermon was preached by his life in his last five or six weeks, after he had been told that he only had days in which to live. He had such confidence of his home in heaven, which Christ had purchased for him. A friend telephoned to ask him of his health, and as it was explained the caller remarked, 'So it's only a matter of time?' 'Yes,' replied the patient, 'but it is for you too, isn't it?'

All of humanity is travelling along a path that leads each individual through the turnstile of death.

Frequently the Bible reminds us of the inevitability of death. King David said, 'But truly, as the Lord lives and as your soul lives, there is but a step between me and death.'[3] We need to understand what God's word has to say about death because we all secretly imagine we will be exempt from its clutches.

A widow who lived in Tekoa wisely said, 'For we will surely die and become like water spilled on the ground, which cannot be gathered up again.'[4]

Suffering Job had the reality of death brought home to him. His groaning can be heard between the lines of much that he uttered.[5]

In the Psalms we read, 'But you shall die like men, and fall like one of the princes.'[6] The 'weeping prophet' Jeremiah cried out, 'For death has come through our windows, has entered our palaces, to kill off the children.'[7]

'And it is appointed for men to die once, but after this the judgment,'[8] says the New Testament.

The apostle Paul wrote to Timothy saying, 'For we brought nothing into this world, and it is certain we can carry nothing out.'[9]

God and we know the date of our birth. Only God knows the date of our death. We have to admit, with the patriarch Isaac, 'I do not know the day of my death.'[10]

There is an old legend about a merchant in Baghdad

who one day sent his servant to the market. Before very long the servant came back, white and trembling, and in great agitation said to his master: 'Down in the market-place I was jostled by a woman in the crowd and when I turned round I saw it was Death that jostled me. She looked at me and made a threatening gesture. Master, please lend me your horse for I must hasten away to avoid her. I will ride to Samara and there I will hide and Death will not find me.'

The merchant lent him his horse and the servant galloped away in great haste.

Later the merchant went down to the market-place and saw Death standing in the crowd. He went over to her and he asked,

'Why did you frighten my servant this morning? Why did you make that threatening gesture?'

Death responded, 'It was not a threatening gesture, it was only a start of surprise. I was astonished to see him in Baghdad for I have an appointment with him tonight in Samara.'

The evangelist D.L. Moody never forgot the childhood memory of hearing the bells of his village church in New England tolling out at funerals the age of the person who was to be buried. It was not always the old, but often there were just thirteen, fourteen or fifteen chimes.

While the Stalins and Hitlers of this world murdered their targetted opponents by the millions, death makes no such discrimination. Death gives no reprieve, but keeps all it has won. Young and old, rich and poor, good and bad, famous and insignificant are captured by this last enemy.

The gift

Secondly, after the diagnosis comes the remedy. After the grave, the verse tells us of the gift—'thanks be to God who gives us the victory.'

The testimony of countless Christians is one of quiet confidence of God's life in them, in life, through death, and on into eternity. This is not based upon the vain delusions such as are often spoken about people at their funerals. Instead, relying on the finished work of Christ, that he died and rose, the Christian has claimed the cleansing that Jesus died to offer, as well as his constant and everlasting companionship.

For the Christian, though death may destroy the body, it cannot touch the soul or spirit. At the moment of Christian conversion there is established an everlasting link between God and the new convert. As Paul wrote:

> For I am persuaded that neither death nor life, nor angels nor principalities nor powers, nor things present nor things to come, nor height nor depth, nor any other created thing, shall be able to separate us from the love of God which is in Christ Jesus our Lord.[11]

'We all have thoughts that would shame even hell' wrote Robert Louis Stevenson. Call it hypocrisy, selfishness, failure or weakness, it is nevertheless the sting of death that is sin. Would there be death at all if there had been no sin? Would anyone fear death if we could pass through it with a clear conscience? Surely not! The unknown of the future may appear daunting, but it is made dreadful because of the known of the past.

If physical death is the separation of the body from the soul, and if there is certainty that the real person is living on for ever with God in heaven, then there need be no fear of leaving and laying aside the body.

Patricia St John is a wonderful writer of Christian

stories for children. She expresses this truth so well in her book *The Tanglewoods' Secret*. Terry, a Christian gypsy boy, has died. His friend Ruth is grieving alone when she meets a wise old yokel called Mr Tandy, whom she questions.

'They buried Terry in the earth and we left him there, and it seemed so sad and lonely. How can Terry be with the Shepherd when we left him lying in the earth?'

The old man did not answer for a moment, and then he started scraping about with his hands in the leaf-fall as though he were looking for something. His search was rewarded and he held out a shiny brown conker in one hand, and an empty seed box in the other—a withered old thing with green prickles turning brown.

'Now tell me,' he said, in his slow, thoughtful voice, 'what's a-goin' to happen to the conker, and what's a-goin' to happen to the covering?'

'Oh,' I answered, 'the case will get buried in the leaves and then I suppose it will just wither away. It isn't needed any more; but the conker will grow roots and leaves and turn into a chestnut tree.'

'That's right,' said Mr Tandy, encouragingly. 'Ye couldn't have said it better; now, tell me this, little maid; when you see the young chestnut tree a-waving its little new leaves in the sunshine next spring, with the birds a-singing round it, and the rain a-watering of it, you ain't goin' to fret any more for that old case what's crumbled under the leaves, be you?'

'No-o,' I answered, with my eyes fixed on his face. Once more I thought I understood.

'Well, then,' said the old man, triumphantly, 'you cease fretting for what you laid below ground—t'weren't nothing but the case. The laddie's a-growing strong in the sunshine up yonder, along of his Saviour.'

His kind old eyes lit up with joy as he spoke; he threw down the conker and case, shouldered his axe and rose stiffly to his feet, because his knees were 'full of rheumatics' as he had once told me. Then he bade me go home.[12]

Jesus' disciple Peter, knowing he was soon to die and leave his body wrote, 'I must put off my tent, just as our Lord Jesus Christ showed me.'[13]

The same truth has been borne out in Christian experience time without number.

Susannah Bicks was a sweet Christian girl. In 1664, aged fourteen, she was about to die in Holland. Her last words were, 'Father, you see that my body is this tabernacle which shall be broken down; my soul shall now depart from it, and shall be taken up to heaven.'

John Newton, converted slave trader and author of the hymn *Amazing Grace*, quaintly said before his death in 1807, 'I am like a person going on a journey in a stagecoach, who expects its arrival every hour, and is frequently looking out of the window for it.... I am packed and sealed, and ready for the post.'

Henry Martyn, missionary to India and Iran and Bible translator, a day or two before his death in 1812 wrote in his diary:

I sat in the orchard and thought with sweet comfort and peace, of my God in solitude—my Companion, my Friend, and Comforter! O, when shall time give place to Eternity? When shall appear that new heaven and new earth wherein dwelleth righteousness? There shall in no wise enter in anything that defileth; none of that wickedness that has made men worse than wild beasts—none of those corruptions that add still more to the miseries of mortality shall be seen or heard any more.

In May 1987, the USS *Stark* was missiled by an Iraqi jet fighter. Thirty-seven American marines died. The front page of *The Times* on 21 May printed a photograph of five-year-old John Kiser, the son of one of the dead sailors. He was standing with his hand on his heart, watching the coffin of his father as it was unloaded at Washington airport.

Mrs Kiser was interviewed by the press. *The Times* reported in the following way:

'I don't have to mourn or wear black because I know my husband's in heaven,' she said. 'I am happy because I know he is better off.'

Later the US Ambassador in Bahrain said that Mrs Kiser and her son had given him a letter and a New Testament, translated into Arabic, to be sent to the pilot of the Iraqi plane.

He would deliver the package, addressed to 'The men who attacked the Stark, Dad's ship', to the Iraqi Ambassador in Bahrain, 'in the hope that he will send it to the pilot to show that even the son...and the wife do not hold any grudge and are at the same time praying for the one who took the life of the father.'

The giver

Thirdly, in this text we see the Giver. He, of course, as we see in the verse, is the Lord Jesus Christ. His gift is of infinite value, for he paid an infinite price to be able to offer it to us all. The cost was not the sacrifice of corruptible things such as silver or gold, but his own precious blood.[14]

The gift, which in this verse is victory in the face of death, also includes forgiveness, new spiritual life, God's power to live day by day, his total presence through all situations, as well as a host of other blessings, which the Scriptures urge believers to revel in. The gift is not to be worked for or earned, or it would cease to be a gift. If we receive our due deserts, we would be lost for ever, 'For the wages of sin is death, but the *gift* of God is eternal life in Christ Jesus our Lord.'[15]

When Christ healed the sick, raised the dead, or taught the multitudes, he did not ask for payment or contribution. People did not have to work to earn his favour. The gospel is always freely given. Christ the giver paid the infinite price, for God was in Christ reconciling the world to himself.

Sin is so serious that it must be punished infinitely and eternally. Either the sinner who is finite (man) must be infinitely punished, or the infinite substitute (Christ) must suffer for a finite length of time. Christ was God manifest in the flesh. In the dark hours on the cross, without sin ever having stained him, Christ became sin for us and carried the guilt that would condemn us eternally.

Christ died so that we might live. He suffered so that we might enjoy his peace. He rose from the dead, defeating death and the grave. Christ laid aside the grave clothes and stepped from an empty tomb with the keys of death and hell firmly gripped in his hand.

A family was enjoying a peaceful picnic until suddenly their little girl began to panic and scream. A bee was flying near to her face. Nothing consoled her until the father stood up and swiped the bee. As he did, it stuck to him and stung him, shook itself and flew away. The father then turned to his daughter and said, 'You're all right now. A bee can only sting once and I have taken the sting in your place.'

Christ did the same. He took the sting of death. He was stung by our sin so that we might be saved from it. He can release us from the power of sin, death and hell to give us life everlasting. He has tasted the bitterness of death for everyone. He died to atone for sins not his own (read Hebrews 2:9–18 and John 8:51,52). A Christian is a person who has received the gift of forgiveness from the giver.

The gratitude

This is the fourth idea found in the verse. We read, 'But thanks be to God...' Christ, having loved us and given himself for us, is such a great and undeserved expression of love that the recipient becomes overwhelmed and overflowing with thankfulness. Paul, the apostle, was so deeply grateful that he said we are not our own, but have been bought with a price. He felt that with just food and clothing he was content because Christ meant so much to him.

Only the Christian can say over the open grave 'Thanks' or 'Victory'. This is not to minimise death. It is still an enemy. Christians grieve. Jesus wept at the tomb of a loved one, even though he knew that he would raise Lazarus back to life. But Christians do not sorrow as others who have no hope.[16]

I remember reading the following poem to a dying Christian friend. Then, seconds before he was in eternity, my wife whispered in his ear, 'John, you will very soon be in the presence of the Lord Jesus. He is altogether lovely.'

Cancer is so limited...
It cannot cripple love,
It cannot shatter hope,
It cannot corrode faith,
It cannot eat away peace,
It cannot destroy confidence,
It cannot kill friendship,
It cannot shut out memories,
It cannot silence courage,
It cannot invade the soul,
It cannot reduce eternal life,
It cannot quench the Spirit,
It cannot lessen the power of the resurrection,
Cancer is so limited.

Have you trusted Christ as Saviour and Lord? Have you yielded all to him, as your natural response to his deserved rights over you? A life lived for self and sin is an expression of ingratitude for his love.

To be absent from this body is to be present with the Lord.[17] Christ said to the dying thief who repented and believed, 'Assuredly, I say to you, today you will be with me in Paradise.'[18]

How different will be the destiny of those who refuse Christ and his gift!

A Salvation Army lady went up to a prostitute standing on the streets in Soho, who was quite abusive to the Salvationist. The lady persisted until she was told to 'Get lost!' Lovingly as she turned away, the lady said, 'My dear, you are lost.' The prostitute never forgot those haunting words so descriptive of her life.

Where will you spend eternity?

Christ who loved so much wooed people to heaven and warned of hell. 'The wicked shall be turned into hell, and all the nations that forget God.'[19] Jesus himself spoke of 'weeping and gnashing of teeth'.[20] He spoke of those on his left hand being commanded, 'Depart from me, you cursed, into the everlasting fire prepared for the devil and his angels.'[21] Perhaps most poignant of all is the story told by Christ in Luke 16. The sugar-sweet Christianity that is prevalent in the West today has often overlooked this striking passage, but if you read it carefully the reality of eternity will be abundantly clear.

Jesus told of a rich man whose rejection of God was shown by his neglect of his neighbour, a poor beggar. One lived on earth in great comfort, the other in such desperation that he longed for the crumbs that fell from the rich man's table. However, in eternity, the rich man was in hell but the beggar, whose name, Lazarus, means 'in God I trust', was with God.[22] In the passage there is no deed such as murder, adultery or robbery. But to leave out God from a life is the greatest of all sins. As C.S. Lewis expressed it, 'The safest road to hell is the gradual one—the gentle slope, soft underfoot, without sudden turnings, without milestones, without signposts.'[23]

Occasionally, the awful horror of man's inhumanity or sinfulness pierces our hearts and emotions. Something within us cries out for justice, sometimes for vengeance. But vengeance belongs to God. He will repay.[24] The sins to which we have grown accustomed, be they thoughts, actions or lack of actions, God has consistently hated, and has always insisted that such wrongdoing must be punished.

The revelation of God (the Bible) and the resurrection of Christ both show that there is life after death. The Bible makes very plain that God will one day judge each individual.[25] There are some who say that everybody will eventually be saved, but the same Greek word in the Bible that speaks of eternal separation from God is used to describe the eternity of heaven.[26] After death there is no second chance. The Bible nowhere teaches purgatory. God's judgement will usher in an everlasting, conscious existence of the soul and personality either in heaven or in hell. C.S. Lewis said, 'Once a man is united to God, how could he not live for ever? Once a man is separated from God, what can he do but wither and die?'

There are many passages in the Bible that teach that there is hell for those who willingly and knowingly reject Christ as Lord and Saviour:

> In flaming fire taking vengeance on those who do not know God, and on those who do not obey the gospel of our Lord Jesus Christ. These shall be punished with everlasting destruction from the presence of the Lord and from the glory of his power.[27]

> I am tormented in this flame.[28]

> But the cowardly, unbelieving, abominable, murderers, sexually immoral, sorcerers, idolaters, and all liars shall have their part in the lake which burns with fire and brimstone, which is the second death.[29]

Can a loving God send a person to hell? The answer is yes, but always reluctantly. People who refused to turn from sin to receive God's mercy and forgiveness condemn themselves. Like a sick patient refusing the doctor's remedy, so many stubbornly resist God's love towards them. God, who is both just and loving, must punish sin.

The resurrection of the Lord Jesus is God's receipt that Christ's payment for sin on the cross has been accepted. Heaven is promised to all who put their trust in Christ:

> Blessed be the God and Father of our Lord Jesus Christ, who according to his abundant mercy has begotten us again to a living hope through the resurrection of Jesus Christ from the dead, to an inheritance incorruptible and undefiled and that does not fade away, reserved in heaven for you, who are kept by the power of God through faith for salvation ready to be revealed in the last time.[30]

The prophet Ezekiel had a vision that has been popularised by the negro spiritual, 'Them bones, them bones, them dry bones!' This is how he described it in chapter 37 of his book:

> The hand of the Lord came upon me and brought me out in the Spirit of the Lord, and set me down in the midst of the valley; and it was full of bones.
>
> Then he caused me to pass by them all around, and behold, there were very many in the open valley; and indeed they were very dry. And he said to me, 'Son of man, can these bones live?'
>
> So I answered, 'O Lord God, you know.'
>
> Again he said to me, 'Prophesy to these bones, and say to them, "O dry bones, hear the word of the Lord! Thus says the Lord God to these bones: 'Surely I will cause breath to enter into you, and you shall live. I will put sinews on you and bring flesh upon you, cover you with skin and put

breath in you; and you shall live. Then you shall know that I am the Lord.' " '

So I prophesied as I was commanded; and as I prophesied, there was a noise, and suddenly a rattling; and the bones came together, bone to bone. Indeed, as I looked, the sinews and the flesh came upon them, and the skin covered them over; but there was no breath in them.

Then he said to me, 'Prophesy to the breath, prophesy, son of man, and say to the breath, "Thus says the Lord God: 'Come from the four winds, O breath, and breathe on these slain, that they may live.' " '

So I prophesied as he commanded me, and breath came into them, and they lived, and stood upon their feet, an exceedingly great army.[31]

He went on to explain that the symbolism pictured the nation of Israel at that time. In God's economic use of words, however, they surely also picture another truth, which is applicable to all.[32]

At the end of time as we know it, there is to be a resurrection of the dead, when spirit and soul, whether with the Lord or lost from him, will be joined again to a resurrection body.

This is not fairy-tale speculation, but a theme running through the Bible. See, for example, in Job:

And after my skin is destroyed, this I know, that in my flesh I shall see God.[33]

In Isaiah we read:

Your dead shall live; together with my dead body they shall arise. Awake and sing, you who dwell in dust; for your dew is like the dew of herbs, and the earth shall cast out the dead.[34]

In Daniel it says:

And many of those who sleep in the dust of the earth shall

awake, some to everlasting life, some to shame and everlasting contempt.[35]

In Matthew's Gospel Jesus said:

And he will send his angels with a great sound of a trumpet, and they will gather together his elect from the four winds, from one end of heaven to the other.[36]

In John's Gospel Christ says:

Whoever eats my flesh and drinks my blood has eternal life, and I will raise him up at the last day.[37]

Paul said in the book of Acts:

I have hope in God, which they themselves also accept, that there will be a resurrection of the dead, both of the just and the unjust.[38]

In 1 Corinthians we read:

So also is the resurrection of the dead. The body is sown in corruption, it is raised in incorruption.[39]

Philippians says:

. . . that I may know him and the power of his resurrection, and the fellowship of his sufferings, being conformed to his death.[40]

The last Bible book, Revelation, describes how:

The sea gave up the dead who were in it, and death and Hades [or hell] delivered up the dead who were in them. And they were judged, each one according to his works.[41]

There is coming a moment when 'grave-breaking' will begin. Ears long since dead will hear the voice of God and perhaps those who have never heard the voice of God before will be 'awakened' on this great day.

As two types of people have lived and died, so two types will rise: those who had trusted Christ and knew God and those who rejected him; those whose trust has been placed in Christ and many who relied on their own good standing and state; those destined to heaven and those destined to hell.

Everyone will rise: the octogenarian and the infant; kings and politicians; both good and bad; great men and beggars; armies of victors and vanquished; men and women murdered by weapons, in fires, by guillotines or who rotted in dungeons; the shipwrecked and the lone victim of the heat of a desert; people buried in great pomp and ceremony and those who were never buried. Millions from the continents and countries of the world will rise at the command of the all-powerful, all-knowing God.

As crystals dissolve in liquid only to reappear when the liquid is heated and evaporates, so the dust of the earth, which once took into itself the body of man, will, on the appointed day, give up its dead.

In eternity, the Christian's resurrection body will be glorious, immortal and powerful. There will be no wrinkles, stoops, grey hairs, deformity, ailments, disease, groans, nor coughs. There will be work without weariness, no night and no need for sleep.

The wrong of the person who neglects or rejects God will appear so great then because it will be seen in the true light.

It is not only some modern-day sceptics who find it hard to comprehend all this teaching. Twenty centuries ago Paul met the same questioning. He answered authoritatively and concluded triumphantly. Read what he wrote to Christians long ago:

But someone will say, 'How are the dead raised up?'...Now this I say, brethren, that flesh and blood cannot inherit the kingdom of God; nor does corruption inherit incorruption. Behold, I tell you a mystery: We shall not all sleep, but we shall all be changed—in a moment, in the twinkling of an eye, at the last trumpet. For the trumpet will sound, and the dead will be raised incorruptible, and we shall be changed. For this corruptible must put on incorruption, and this mortal must put on immortality. So when this corruptible has put on incorruption, and this mortal has put on immortality, then shall be brought to pass the saying that is written: 'Death is swallowed up in victory.'

'O Death, where is your sting?

O Hades, where is your victory?'

The sting of death is sin, and the strength of sin is the law. But thanks be to God, who gives us the victory through our Lord Jesus Christ. Therefore, my beloved brethren, be steadfast, immovable, always abounding in the work of the Lord, knowing that your labour is not in vain in the Lord.[42]

Do you know the Christ who has defeated death and who is willing to live within you as Lord and cleanse you as Saviour?

Notes

1. Ecclesiastes 12:7.
2. 1 Corinthians 15:56.
3. 1 Samuel 20:3.
4. 2 Samuel 14:14.
5. Job 7:1–3, for example.
6. Psalm 82:7.
7. Jeremiah 9:21.
8. Hebrews 9:27.
9. 1 Timothy 6:7.
10. Genesis 27:2.
11. Romans 8:38,39.
12. Patricia St John, *The Tanglewoods' Secret* (Scripture Union, 1948, p.146). Used by permission; all rights reserved.
13. 2 Peter 1:14.

14. 1 Peter 1:18,19.
15. Romans 6:23.
16. 1 Thessalonians 4:13.
17. 2 Corinthians 5:8.
18. Luke 23:43.
19. Psalm 9:17.
20. Matthew 22:13.
21. Matthew 25:41.
22. Luke 16:19–31.
23. *The Screwtape Letters* (Fount Paperbacks, 1982).
24. Romans 12:19.
25. 2 Corinthians 5:10; Hebrews 9:27; Revelation 20:11–15.
26. Matthew 25:46.
27. 2 Thessalonians 1:8,9.
28. Luke 16:24.
29. Revelation 21:8. See also Matthew 13:41,42,49,50; 25:41; Mark 9:42–48; Revelation 14:10,11; 20:14,15.
30. 1 Peter 1:3–5.
31. Ezekiel 37:1–10.
32. See Galatians 4:24, 'which things are symbolic...'.
33. Job 19:26.
34. Isaiah 26:19.
35. Daniel 12:2.
36. Matthew 24:31.
37. John 6:54.
38. Acts 24:15.
39. 1 Corinthians 15:42.
40. Philippians 3:10.
41. Revelation 20:13.
42. 1 Corinthians 15:35, 50–58.

6

Why Believe Christians Are Children of God?

*But as many as received him [Christ], to them he gave
the right to become children of God.*
John 1:12

There is a creative instinct in each person. After all, we
were made in the image of the Creator God. So, if you
were able to create a man, what sort of being would you
come up with?

No doubt, he would have a physical dimension. Each
one produced would have a unique body with size and
shape. The body is important, but not all-important.
Every few weeks I have part of mine amputated. But I
don't weep as the barber sweeps up the cuttings! They
are only a part of my body.

I heard a doctor explain that the body contains
enough lime to whitewash a hen coop, enough iron to
make a nail, enough phosphorous to tip 2,200 matches,
enough sulphur to rid a dog of fleas, enough potash to
blow up a toy car, enough sugar to sweeten six cups of
tea, enough fat to make seven bars of soap—and the
whole lot is worth only a few pounds.

We all know that there is more to us than a mere
conglomeration of atoms and cells. The body is like a
shell or casing, which houses the real person.

Would you also make man with intellectual ability?
Surely our facility to reason and act reasonably is one of

our greatest attributes. Four centuries ago Galileo Galilei rightly said, 'I do not feel obliged to believe that the same God who has endowed us with sense, reason and intellect has intended us to forego their use!' We are able with the use of our brain to be analytical, conceptional, intuitive, artistic and verbal.

What an awful individual, though, would be a man with great intelligence, yet who had no feelings, emotions or heart. Man is more than a body-with-a-mind.

Would you as well make man a social being? One of the great joys of human existence is the ability to socialise. Interaction with the opposite sex and companions of the same sex may be delightful or at times disturbing, but it is part of our *raison d'être*. We are social beings and were formed for society. As God created the earth and everything in it at the beginning of time, he repeatedly saw that 'it was good'.[1] The first time he said something was not good was when, having created Adam, he stated, 'It is not good that man should be alone.'[2]

Is that all that there would be to your created man? Would you not also want to impart something of your life into his? When God created man he made him higher than any other form of life—vegetable or animal. Humans have a spiritual dimension to their existence. We read in Genesis, 'Then God said, "Let us make man in our own image"';[3] 'And the Lord God formed man of the dust of the ground, and breathed into his nostrils the breath of life; and man became a living being.'[4] Henry Jacobson expressed the thought well: 'Like animals, man is a creature of earth; unlike them he can become a citizen of heaven.' Man has the ability to know, appreciate, enjoy and worship God. The life of the living God can live in the life of a human being. The dust of man was created to be filled with the deity of the Creator.

There was a time when God and man walked together in the garden in the cool of the day. There was a harmonious relationship unspoilt by the sin or selfishness of man. The spiritual part of the new creation was alive and well. Man and woman were complete, enjoying their God, each other and the world around them.

But man was not created as a puppet on a string or an electronic robot. He was made with the challenge, freedom and responsibility of the ability to make choices. Instead of obeying God, there was a deliberate act of rebellion. It was never God's desire for man to discover evil, whatever its source, but Adam and Eve took the fruit of the tree of the knowledge of good and evil.

Man and woman had been made so intricately in the image of God that the least flaw would transform them into the very image of the devil. As a result of their sin, paradise lost was now their domain. Their spiritual nature died, so that all born of man and woman since have been born spiritually dead. Immediately, we see Adam and Eve on the run from God, who himself took the initiative in tenderly seeking them: 'Then the Lord God called to Adam and said to him, "Where are you?"'[5]

How many millions have been born since? Different colours and cultures, backgrounds and beliefs, personalities and parentage form the vast array of the teeming multitudes. All are alike in that their greatest need is to be reconciled to God so that they might be made spiritually alive. We were made with a physical, intellectual, social and spiritual dimension, but with that spiritual nature dead, man is incomplete.

Not all are as outwardly wicked as others. Jesus himself spoke of it being more tolerable on judgement day for some than for others, though all the groups of which he spoke were nevertheless lost from God.[6]

Philosophers and theologians have in past times argued that there are, as it were, different kinds of existence. These are nothing to do with class or status, but attitudes and actions.

The lowest level of human existence (let us call it level one) is the type of person who is guided by nothing but his own desires. If this person has any urge, he follows his 'instinct' to fulfil these desires. His motto is summarised by the common expression, 'If it feels good, do it.' He is guided by his impulses, passions and lusts. He will do anything to satisfy and gratify his physical desires or his perverted mind. Though often described by onlookers as behaving like an animal, that is far from the truth. Such a person was made to know God, but sin has not only devastated the spiritual dimension he was created to enjoy, but ruined every other part of him.

Spiritual death brings with it 'soulish' death and ultimately leads to physical death.

Sadly some in this category have gone down in the world's hall of infamy and have become household names for their wickedness.

The Bible describes such people in passages such as Galatians 5, verses 19 to 21, which says:

> Now the works of the flesh are evident, which are: adultery, fornication, uncleanness, licentiousness, idolatry, sorcery, hatred, contentions, jealousies, outbursts of wrath, selfish ambitions, dissensions, heresies, envy, murders, drunkenness, revelries, and the like; of which I tell you beforehand, just as I also told you in time past, that those who practise such things will not inherit the kingdom of God.

On a higher level (level two) is the vast majority of the population. These are the crowd followers. They are enslaaved by soap operas on television, buy what is advertised because everybody else is buying it, and their conversation is inconsequential and trivial. Their views and politics are determined solely by what is expressed by their peers, in their newspaper and on television and radio. They do not think individually and would never take a lone stand against current trends or their peer group. They are basically pawns manipulated by the media. As Scripture says, they are 'futile in their thoughts, and their foolish hearts [are] darkened.'[7] They may be pleasant people who seek to be kind and helpful, but they are not the folk they were originally created to be.

Perhaps the third level is the group of people who are governed by reason. Their constant appeal is to common sense. They have a conscience and earnestly seek to follow it, even if it is a costly stand for them. These have been prominent in the news because they have often been 'thorns in the flesh' of corrupt or inept governments, totalitarian regimes or dictatorial tyrants. Their logic, knowledge, insight and courage may be admirable, but they still fall short of the glory for which man was created.

All these three levels describe 'natural' people instead of 'spiritual' men and women. Some may even be religious, but they do not enjoy a personal relationship with their Creator. They do not know God.

There is, however, a fourth level, whereby the individual is guided by the Spirit of the living God and indwelt by him. Such people have each come to a moment in their lives when they have asked Christ to cleanse them of past sin, and by his Holy Spirit to actually come as a welcome holy guest to dwell in their lives, to take control of them and bring them into an intimate relationship with God. He, through their mind and reason, guides them. They in turn daily seek to bring their life, feelings, actions and will under the control of God. They are experiencing what one described as 'the life of God in the soul of man'.

Examples of becoming a child of God

Becoming a son or daughter of God is nothing to do with social class or background. Neither is it the case that these people were born with a religious 'bent'! Nor is the spiritual life something that is attained, earned or

worked up to. It is received as a *gift* from God. There is
not a slow evolution from level one to two to three to
four, but rather a miracle from heaven itself in the life of
men and women whose only qualification is that they are
sinners. 'This is a faithful saying and worthy of all acceptance, that Christ Jesus came into the world to save
sinners, of whom I am chief,'[8] said the apostle Paul. 'I
did not come to call the righteous, but sinners, to repentance,'[9] the Lord Jesus said. The negro spiritual
expresses the same truth from the point of view of the
sinner with the words, 'It's me, it's me, it's me, O Lord,
standing in the need of prayer.'

John Newton had become a 'level one' individual. His
life appeared to be one long drama. Son of an English
sea captain, John went to sea at eleven years of age, and
eventually became a slave-ship captain during the worst
years in the traffic in black slaves when inhuman treat-
ment of negroes was legal and normal. His language and
life betrayed his savage mind. His own epitaph on his
grave in Olney, Buckinghamshire describes him as an
infidel and libertine. Here is how he describes, in eight-
eenth century English, what led to his conversion:

I went to bed that night in my usual security and indif-
ference, but was awakened from a sound sleep by the force
of a violent sea, which broke on board us; so much of it
came down below as filled the cabin I lay in with water. This
alarm was followed by a cry from the deck, that the ship was
going down or sinking.... Another person went up [and]
was instantly washed overboard. We had no leisure to
lament him, nor did we expect to survive him long; for we
soon found the ship was filling with water very fast. The sea
had torn away the upper timbers on one side, and made a
mere wreck in a few minutes. Taking in all circumstances, it
was astonishing, and almost miraculous, that any of us
survived to relate the story.... We expended most of our
clothes and bedding to stop the leaks.... I told one of [my
companions], that in a few days, this distress would serve us
to talk over a glass of wine; but he being a less hardened

sinner than myself, replied, with tears, 'No; it is too late now.' About nine o'clock...just as I was returning from seeing the captain, I said almost without any meaning, 'If this will not do, the Lord have mercy upon us.' This (though spoken with little reflection) was the first desire I had breathed for mercy for the space of many years. I was instantly struck with my own words; and, it directly occurred, 'What mercy can there be for me!' I was obliged to return to the pump, and there I continued till noon, almost every passing wave breaking over my head; but we made ourselves fast with ropes, that we might not be washed away. Indeed, I expected that every time the vessel descended in the sea, she would rise no more; and though I dreaded death now, and my heart foreboded the worst, if the scriptures, which I had long since opposed, were indeed true; yet still I was but half convinced, and remained for a space of time in a sullen frame, a mixture of despair and impatience. I thought, if the Christian religion was true, I could not be forgiven.[10]

But forgiven he was. His cry for mercy was heard. The ship sailed on and he was saved. He had the desire to see his life transformed. He came into contact with other Christians, and was eventually to leave sailing and the slave trade to become an Anglican clergyman.

This blasphemer was the author of hymns such as:

How sweet the name of Jesus sounds
In a believer's ear....

as well as the hymn that will not die:

Amazing grace, how sweet the sound
That saved a wretch like me.
I once was lost, but now am found,
Was blind but now I see.

He was taken from level one to level four in an instant of time. His faint cry for mercy was heard by the one whose ear is not heavy that it cannot hear.[11] John Newton was sincere in his repentance and faith towards Christ, and so he was forgiven and given spiritual life.

As far as level two is concerned, there are countless millions of people who, though unknown as far as the world is concerned, are known to God. John Newton lived two hundred years ago. Quite recently, Alf and Sandra Tipper of Leigh in Lancashire found that Newton's God could become theirs. Alf, a laundry manager told their story in the 1988 United Beach Mission magazine:

> It was the first real holiday for my wife, Sandra, and our two children, Becky and Alex. It was also our first visit to picturesque St Ives in Cornwall, and the first time we ever saw a United Beach Mission Team....
>
> The children enjoyed the games and competitions, and like all good holidays it seemed to be over all too soon. I vividly remember setting off on the long journey home with two happy little voices singing, 'He made the stars to shine' from the back seat of the car until they fell asleep.
>
> We enjoyed that holiday so much that we booked again at St Ives for the next two years in succession, and each time the United Beach Mission was there. We chatted to the team on the beach, and stopped to listen in the evenings as they held their open-air meetings at the harbour.
>
> Sandra has always believed in God, had gone regularly to church as a girl and had taught in Sunday school before getting married. She had always thought herself as much a Christian as anyone else. It was a shock to realise, as she listened to the message, that she was not a Christian at all! Despite her religious background she had never known God personally for herself, or given him any place in her life.
>
> One team member gave her a copy of John's Gospel and asked her to promise to read one chapter a day until she had read it all. In fact, that same night in our holiday flat she read it straight through, not putting it down until she had read every word. She told me later, 'There were tears in my eyes as I realised that Jesus had died on that cross for me. Jesus had taken my punishment, and now I had a chance to

'start again'. I saw myself as I really was—stubborn, selfish, and guilty before God. So in the privacy of that bedroom I prayed and asked God to take over my life and make me a better person. The next morning I woke up and realised that I now knew what being a Christian really meant—I had become one!'

When we returned home I soon noticed a change in Sandra—for one thing, she never seemed to stop talking about God and he seemed so real to her! She read her Bible, prayed, and wanted to go to church—things she was not doing before! I liked this 'new' Sandra, and we began to attend regularly as a family at a local Bible-believing church. On the beach I had been cynical, dismissing the team as 'religious nuts'. On more than one occasion I had pretended to be asleep to avoid having to talk to them! But underneath it all, I knew that they were right. I had a foul mouth and a foul temper, and I was ashamed of my life when I compared it with theirs. I knew that unless I did something about it, I was lost.

In the November of that year we were invited to a bonfire party at the home of some Christian friends we had met on the beach mission. They had a peace and contentment in their lives that really showed, and I knew it was lacking in mine. I wasn't singing with them, and I knew why—I wasn't part of them because I didn't know God for myself as they did. By the dying embers of that bonfire I silently asked God to become real to me too and change me. I believe he did answer that prayer, because ever since then I have been aware of him in a way I never knew before.

All this happened some years ago now. You might ask, has becoming a Christian worked? Has it lasted? As to how much God has changed our lives, others must be the judge. All we can say is that we still feel the same about him, and have never lost that sense of a personal, living relationship, and we still attend church as a family.

Ordinary people, on level two, met the extraordinary God and were taken to level four of humanity.

A former professor of medieval and Renaissance literature at Cambridge University, and prolific author, is my example of a level three man. C.S. Lewis was for many years an atheist, but he relates, 'In the Trinity Term of 1929 I gave in, and admitted God was God...perhaps the most dejected and reluctant convert in all England.'

In his autobiography, *Surprised by Joy*,[12] he describes his feelings at the time of conversion:

The odd thing was that before God closed in on me, I was in fact offered what now appears a moment of wholly free choice. In a sense. I was going up Headington Hill on the top of a bus. Without words and (I think) almost without images, a fact about myself was somehow presented to me. I became aware that I was holding something at bay, or shutting something out. Or, if you like, that I was wearing some stiff clothing, like corslets, or even a suit of armour, as if I were a lobster. I felt myself being, there and then, given a free choice. I could open the door or keep it shut; I could unbuckle the armour or keep it on. Neither choice was presented as a duty; no threat or promise was attached to either, though I knew that to open the door or to take off the corslet meant the incalculable. The choice appeared to be momentous but it was also strangely unemotional. I was moved by no desires or fears. In a sense I was not moved by anything. I chose to open, to unbuckle, to loosen the rein. I say, 'I chose,' yet it did not really seem possible to do the opposite. On the other hand, I was aware of no motives. You could argue that I was not a free agent, but I am more inclined to think that this came nearer to being a perfectly free act than most that I have ever done. Necessity may not be the opposite of freedom, and perhaps a man is most free when, instead of producing motives, he could only say, 'I am what I do.' Then came the repercussion on the imaginative level. I felt as if I were a man of snow at long last beginning to melt. The melting was starting in my back—drip-drip and presently trickle-trickle. I rather disliked the feeling.

Academic prowess was not sufficient to satisfy the God-shaped gulf in the life of C.S. Lewis. Only God could fill that.

Has such a moment of Christian conversion ever happened to you? Has your sin been forgiven? Are you right with God? Do you have spiritual life? Are you certain of heaven? Are you a child of God?

Marks of a child of God

The apostle Paul had not yet visited the city of Rome, the capital of the Roman Empire, when he wrote to the group of believers who were living there. He was concerned that they should fully grasp the essence of Christian belief, so in his letter to the Romans, in the New Testament, he straightforwardly outlines the gospel message. In chapter 8, verses 14 to 17, he lists some of the characteristics of sonship or what are marks of being a child of God.

A child of God belongs to God (verse 15)

He can actually talk to God as his Father. There is a family tie. Nothing can separate a Christian from the love of God. After all, Christ actually died out of love for people. If, then, a person receives the gift of forgiveness, how warm will be the welcome, and how real the relationship between God and the new family member.

A child of God will talk to God (verse 15)

He will pray. Prayer is not just an emergency rip-cord to pull in times of great extremity; it is the means of speaking to God our Father. Prayer is the life-line between God and man. It is the spontaneous consequence of a new bond established by Christ himself.

If you never pray, ask yourself, 'Am I really converted?' God reassured Ananias that Saul of Tarsus had truly been converted with words, 'behold, he is praying.'[13] Even the weakest Christian will want to start to pray with a few words of thanksgiving, praise, confession of sin and requests to God.

Why Believe?

A child of God knows his heavenly Father (verse 16)

The Christian relationship with God is not casual or platonic. There is a knowledge of God that goes so deep that it stimulates an ever-growing desire for more of God. Can a cross-Channel swimmer claim to know the English Channel? Maybe, but there is so much more than twenty-three miles in a more or less straight line. There is the vastness of the sea with which to become familiar. In like manner, though the Christian knows God, it will be a lifelong desire to know God more and more. He is not a dull personality with whom one quickly tires, but the infinite God whose loving person is such that he stirs within the Christian a heart that hungers and thirsts after the living God.

A child of God will want to walk with God (verse 14)

If he loved us enough not to spare his own Son but freely delivered him up for us (verse 32), then we can implicitly trust him. God guides those who are guidable. He has general desires for all and specific plans for each individual who trusts him. As Christians, we will not want to rush ahead like a horse, or lag behind like a mule, but simply walk with God, at his pace and in his direction.

A child of God is called to suffer (verse 17)

Jesus said, 'If anyone desires to come after me, let him deny himself, and take up his cross daily and follow me.'[14]

God said of Saul of Tarsus, who had just been converted, 'He is a chosen vessel of mine to bear my name before Gentiles, kings, and the children of Israel. For I will show him how many things he must suffer for my name's sake.'[15] Paul himself wrote, 'All who desire to live godly in Christ Jesus will suffer persecution.'[16] A Christian is swimming against prevailing tides and trends. The world is at enmity with God and will be at enmity with those who are his friends and family. When all speak well of us, we will need to examine very carefully our relationship with God. When God is the one we seek to please, those who keep God out of their thinking will not be pleased.

A child of God is an heir (verse 17)

Finally, God is the Father of all who truly believe. All that is his is ours. Jesus promised that the meek shall inherit the earth.[17] Through Christ's work on the cross, and the Holy Spirit's work in us, God has made Christian people his own for ever. In fact, the Holy Spirit *guarantees* our inheritance (read Ephesians 1:13,14 and 2 Corinthians 1:21 and 5:5). What an inheritance he is. There are many exceedingly great and precious promises throughout the Bible in which God assures his people that he works all things together for good, overruling evil and undertaking for his sons and daughters.

Becoming a child of God

How then can a person become a part of God's family? We are not children of God by birth. We are all created by him, but need to be brought into his family.

Jesus talked about 'being born again', or being 'born from above'.[18] This involves a completely new start. It is a change in nature, that God brings about in the heart of an individual. The Bible also speaks of adoption:

> But when the fullness of time had come, God sent forth his Son, born of a woman, born under the law, to redeem those who were under the law, that we might receive the adoption as sons. And because you are sons, God has sent forth the Spirit of his Son into your hearts, crying out, 'Abba, Father!'[19]

The word 'adoption' is used because it teaches that we once belonged to someone other than God, but now there has been a change in our position before God. We have a standing before him as sons and daughters, if we have trusted Christ.

The phrase 'born again' has caught the imagination of people in recent years. Advertisers, politicians and preachers have used the term. It originated when, under the cover of darkness, a religious leader approached Jesus Christ with a statement that would have flattered or fooled a lesser man. 'Rabbi,' said Nicodemus to Christ, 'we know that you are a teacher come from God; for no one can do these signs that you do unless God is with him.'

Jesus simply replied, 'Most assuredly, I say to you, unless one is born again, he cannot see the kingdom of God.'

Understandably, Nicodemus, despite the fact that he had great theological training and was renowned for his ability with things religious, was bewildered. In the quietness of the night, he took his opportunity to question Christ further. There was no proud cover-up of ignorance, rather an honest seeking, as Nicodemus continued:

> 'How can a man be born when he is old? Can he enter a second time into his mother's womb and be born?' Jesus answered, 'Most assuredly, I say to you, unless one is born of water and the Spirit, he cannot enter the kingdom of God. That which is born of the flesh is flesh, and that which is born of the Spirit is spirit. Do not marvel that I said to you, "You must be born again." The wind blows where it wishes, and you hear the sound of it, but cannot tell where it comes from and where it goes. So is everyone who is born of the Spirit.'[20]

The nineteenth century preacher Henry Drummond had a helpful illustration of what it means to be born again. He said that there are many levels of 'kingdoms' in this world: from the lowest, the mineral kingdom, to the vegetable kingdom, the animal kingdom, the human kingdom and the highest, God's kingdom. He then argued that it is a basic law of the universe that no kingdom can lift itself up to a higher level. For example, a stone cannot become a rose. A rose, likewise, cannot become a rabbit. A rabbit cannot become a human, and no human can become God. However, it is also a basic law of the universe that each kingdom can reach down and pull a lower one up. For example, the vegetable kingdom can reach down into the mineral kingdom and turn it into grass. From the animal kingdom a cow can chew the grass and turn it into flesh. Then the butcher turns the cow's flesh into steak, which is eaten by a human, so that what is animal becomes human.

God through Christ has come to this world and can reach down to lift us up. Now humans can be 'born from above' or 'born again'.

All of us have been born of water. That was our physical birth. But there needs to be a new birth, which is the start of spiritual life.

Note first that Jesus said, 'You *must* be born again.' Nicodemus was deeply religious, strictly following disciplines of prayer, devoutly seeking to keep religious law, yet still he had to be born again. Indeed, no matter how hard any of us may try to understand spiritual things, we simply *cannot* receive them until we have been born again of the Spirit. Paul explains this in his first letter to the Corinthian Christians, chapter 2, verses 6 to 16. There is no spiritual life until the new birth: there is no everlasting life unless there is a new birth. New birth is the only passport to heaven. How many times I have asked people if they are certain of heaven, only to be told, 'I hope so! I've never done anybody any harm.' I always feel, 'Who is fooling whom?' We all do harm. We are all guilty of sin, which keeps us from God and would condemn us to hell. The only hope lies in the fact that Jesus taught that there is a new birth.

Has this ever happened to you? Have you been born again?

Secondly, you *may* be born again. Jesus said, 'And this is the condemnation, that the light has come into the world, and men loved darkness rather than light, because their deeds were evil.'[21] Those who are lost from God are guilty of deliberately resisting all the obstacles that God would put in the path of those heading to a lost eternity.

Be careful—the day you stopped attending Sunday school, refused to pray, blasphemed, tore up a Christian leaflet given to you, may be the day you finally refused Christ. But you may yet be born again. Christ has done his utmost for you.

He left heaven, coming to this earth in the form of a helpless baby. His express mission was to go to the cross. Far greater than any work of demonstrating power over the devil, disease, disaster or death, was his work of carrying on his shoulders the guilt and sin of all. Few in ancient history are known to us today, but all are known to God. We read of thousands of millions alive today, but God took the sin of every continent and country, and each man and woman, laying it on the Lord Jesus. 'All we like sheep have gone astray; we have turned, every one, to his own way; and the Lord has laid on him the iniquity of us all.'[22]

Let me illustrate this vital aspect of the Christian message.

Quite a few years ago I used to be a teacher in a boys' secondary modern school. It was quite a school! I really enjoyed teaching there. It was in the days when there was corporal punishment in most schools.

One day, in a particular class, I was being questioned by some boys. They were asking me about my Christian beliefs and I remember explaining to them that I really did believe that Christ had died to pay for our sins. After the lesson an Indian boy, a pleasant character, came up to me and asked, 'Sir, how could Christ die for our sins?' Then later he said, 'I don't see how Christ could pay for my sins as I wasn't born.'

I explained how that with God there is no time. He can see the past, the present and the future and he looked forward in time to see us and he took our sin and laid it on Christ. He actually bore the punishment for the wrong we had done so we could be forgiven.

He said, 'I can't believe that,' and we continued discussing things for about twenty-five minutes. It was all very amicable.

It would have been the end of the incident except that about three weeks later I was teaching and he was in the class again, but this time was misbehaving. I repeatedly warned him as I told him to behave. However, he carried on misbehaving. At the end of the lesson there was an incident with a boy seated next to him so I told the trouble-maker to come to the front. 'Do you deserve to be slippered?' I asked. I had a slipper, which I used as a punishment for the boys. He replied, 'Well I suppose I do, sir.' So I said, 'Right, bend over.' I lifted up his blazer and was about to slipper him. Suddenly, I remembered that this was the very lad who had asked me, 'How could Christ die for our sins?' So, instead of slippering him, I said, 'Stand up. You have done wrong, but instead of me slippering you, I'm going to pass the slipper over to you. I'll bend over and you can slipper me as hard as I would have punished you.'

Well, of course, he and the class were delighted at the thought of this. I bent over and he got the slipper and he really did get me right on the 'seat of learning'! Then I stood up, turned to him and said, 'Look, you did wrong, you deserved to be punished, but I took your punishment in your place. Do you remember that question of a few weeks before? How could Christ die for our sin? In a much greater way when the Lord Jesus Christ was on the cross he didn't just take our slippering; he took our sin and all the consequences of it, and he took the punishment so that we could be set free and forgiven.'

Raising Christ from the dead was God's seal on the work of paying the penalty for sin, which Christ did on the cross. Now to each person who will turn in repentance and faith to Christ, God offers forgiveness, new birth, new life and his everlasting presence.

A mischievous boy went up to a Yorkshire yokel with a bird in his hand. 'Sir,' he asked, 'is this bird dead or alive?'

The wise yokel thought, 'If I say it's alive the boy will clench his hand and crush the bird to death. If, however, I say it's dead, the boy will open his hand and let the bird fly away free.'

The man gave his considered answer: 'Whether that bird is dead or alive depends entirely upon you.'

So too, you have the responsibility: either to reject or to receive Christ. If you will, with God's strength, turn from your sin and trust Christ to forgive and live in you, then God will work a wonderful miracle within you. You will be born again. Spiritual and eternal life will be yours. You will be part of God's family for ever. If you refuse him, your heart will harden further against God, and who knows how long God will continue to give you opportunities to trust him?

Last of all note, this is the *moment* to be born again. God makes no promises about tomorrow. Life is short and uncertain. Even if we have a heart still ticking and mind still functioning, there is no guarantee that he will still be speaking to us or that our hearts will be inclined towards him. 'Behold, now is the accepted time; behold, now is the day of salvation.'[23]

There is a legend about the devil interviewing for a junior. He had short-listed three demons. To each he asked, 'What would you do to prevent people trusting

Christ?' The first replied that he would say that there is no God, and the second that there is no judgement. The devil was not content with either of these, feeling that they were not sufficiently convincing. Then he asked the third the same question. The reply came thus: 'I would tell them that there is no hurry.' This demon well understood the urgency of God's call to mankind. He was taken on instantly!

Procrastination is the thief of time and of eternity. It is well said that the road to hell is paved with good intentions. I urge you this very day to take the most important step in your life. Ask God to cleanse you from sin, and ask him to be your Lord and Saviour today. If you are genuinely repentant and trusting, then God will give you a new birth and spiritual life. He will lift you to a new plane of life and begin the process of making you into the person you were created to be.

> But as many as received him, to them he gave the right to become children of God, even to those who believe in his name: who were born, not of blood, nor of the will of the flesh, nor of the will of man, but of God.[24]

Notes

1. Genesis 1:10,12,18,21,25.
2. Genesis 2:18.
3. Genesis 1:26.
4. Genesis 2:7.
5. Genesis 3:9.
6. Matthew 10:15; 11:21–24.
7. Romans 1:21.
8. 1 Timothy 1:15.
9. Matthew 9:13.
10. Richard Cecil (ed.), *The Works of the Rev. John Newton* (New York: Robert Carter Co., 1844, I: p.95 ff.).
11. Isaiah 59:1.

12. C.S. Lewis, *Surprised by Joy* (Fount Paperbacks, Collins, 1955, p.179). Used with permission.
13. Acts 9:11.
14. Luke 9:23.
15. Acts 9:15,16.
16. 2 Timothy 3:12.
17. Matthew 5:5.
18. John 3:3.
19. Galatians 4:4–6.
20. John 3:4–8.
21. John 3:19.
22. Isaiah 53:6.
23. 2 Corinthians 6:2.
24. John 1:12,13.

7

Why Believe Jesus Is the Only Way To God?

Jesus said: *I am the way, the truth and the life. No one comes to the Father except through me.*
John 14:6

The sun was riding high in a Mexican sky. Hundreds of people were gathered at the foot of the ancient pyramid. It was AD 1300. Since early morning they had been waiting anxiously for the great event. By the sundial it was almost time! Suddenly a great shout arose; for as they gazed as far as they could see across the lake, they saw a little boat coming their way. As the boat approached they could discern the figure of a young Indian, handsome, athletic, in the prime of life. As this young Indian slowly paddled his boat to the sandy beach, the jewels on his magnificent garment glistened in the sunlight. Slowly and deliberately, with a dead-pan expression, he made his way through a path that the crowd gladly made for him, toward the pyramid, while garlands of tropical flowers were thrown for his path. Scores knelt and cried, 'Take my sins...Take my sins...Take my sins' or 'Remember me...Remember me...Remember me.'

Just as he reached the stone steps leading to the summit, priests came and quickly stripped him of all his garments. Blue, white, red and yellow paint was put on his body. After preparation and more prayers, alone he slowly climbed the hundred steps. The crowd waited anxiously, breathlessly, excitedly. At last he reached the top. Out of nowhere stepped six priests. Quickly four gripped each limb of his body and quickly bent him over a convex stone. A fifth held his head. A sixth priest had a long, curved, jewelled knife, sharp as a razor's edge. Looking toward the small temple erected on the top of the pyramid and gazing at the face of the stone-carved god, the Indian chanted a few syllables. Like a flash the knife pierced the heart of the young man. A skilful twist and the heart was out.

Each priest reached madly into the place where the heart had been and sprinkled his face with the warm blood. The heart, still palpitating, was rubbed over the face of the image. The twitching body was thrown, head first, over the side of the pyramid. A mad scramble followed. Knives flashed. Each person scrambled to get a piece of flesh to take home for use in a 'communion service' that would bring added blessing.

The sun was sinking over the western horizon when the crowd melted in the distance. Each felt that his sins were forgiven and that the evils that had come upon himself or his family were now atoned for. This was not an unusual scene to the ancient Aztecs, for it happened somewhere in their domain every day. They had eighteen months of twenty days each on their calendar, and each day there were many gods and goddesses to receive sacrifices. Thus twenty thousand human beings a year were slaughtered on the altars of ancient Mexico.

These ancient people engaged in constant warfare to get their sacrificial victims from neighbouring tribes and nations, for the victim sacrificed must be innocent of the particular sins and evils that were to be atoned for. Thus he must come from outside the realm. He must be young and without blemish. For many months before the sacrifice he was carefully trained and was treated in many respects as a god. He was the substitute bearing the sins of the people.'

So began one of evangelist Billy Graham's early, graphic sermons.[1]

Man is incurably religious. Perverted and perverse though religious practices may be, in every part of the globe people 'worship'.

The recent growth in cults and Eastern religions has

been phenomenal. But this is nothing new. Ever since Cain killed Abel[2] there has been a basic divide between those who hope that their works and behaviour will please and placate their god, and those who have relied on and rested in the work of a substitute to cleanse them from sin and bring them to God.

Sincerity may be the hallmark of many religious people, but that is not enough. A sincere person taking poison instead of medicine, genuinely believing that the dose will cure him, is not thereby immune from that chemical's fatal effect. The apostle Paul said the same thing when he wrote:

> For I bear them [the religious people of his day] witness that they have a zeal for God, but not according to knowledge. For they being ignorant of God's righteousness, and seeking to establish their own righteousness, have not submitted to the righteousness of God.[3]

From the beginning, God provided a way for man to have fellowship with his Creator. Rather than an idea of an evolution of religion (starting with a fear of spirits, then progressing to polytheism, followed by monotheism until the present stage of familiarity with God), God has actually stepped into his creation and revealed himself to man.

At first there were shadowy ideas and prophetic pictures and practices in this revelation. This culminated in the coming of Christ, the promised Messiah. He, by his life, death and resurrection, put the finishing strokes to the background picture of all that had been anticipated throughout the Old Testament period.

Man's many methods of groping and grovelling his way back to God are in vain. God has taken the initiative and condescended to reach us.

Most, if not all, religions believe in the existence of a supreme being, with whom they hope, by various means, to make contact, if not in this world then in a world or existence to come. Very often their life's endeavours are all for that very purpose.

There will be elements of truth in any religion that survives. There will be devotees to particular religious systems who will speak of the help they feel they have received from their religion. Some of that may be humanly inexplicable and appear supernatural.

Let us be quite clear that whatever the differences in belief, the real Christian will want to show love and compassion to people whatever their religious views. After all, it was while we were enemies of God that Christ died for us![4] Jesus' parable of the good Samaritan is as applicable for today as for any other generation. However, Christians will find that there is profound disagreement with many of the teachings of systems that demote or exclude Christ. But, in the name of Christ, the Christian will want to obey the Lord Jesus who said:

> You have heard that it was said, 'You shall love your neighbour and hate your enemy.' But I say to you, love your enemies, bless those who curse you, do good to those who hate you, and pray for those who spitefully use you and persecute you, that you may be sons of your Father in heaven; for he makes his sun rise on the evil and on the good, and sends rain on the just and on the unjust. For if you love those who love you, what reward have you? Do not even the tax collectors do the same? And if you greet your brethren only, what do you do more than others? Do not even the tax collectors do so?[5]

Jesus taught the duty of his followers to give food to the hungry, drink to the thirsty, loving care to the 'stranger', clothing to the naked, attention to the sick and timely visits to the prisoners.[6]

When I am asked, 'Haven't more wars been fought over religion than anything else?' my mind goes back to such passages. How can a real Christian fight with someone simply because there are 'religious differences'?

Sadly, just as the cloak of Christ was gambled for at the cross, and then presumably worn by somebody to whom it did not belong, so too, the name of Christ has often been taken by those to whom it does not belong, who have 'worn' it and abused it. If, going directly against your instructions, I murdered in your name, are you to blame? Surely not! A Christian will feel deeply that all need to come to Christ in repentance and faith, but they are not going to fight someone who doesn't! Rather they will want to love that person all the more.

As we seek to demonstrate in other chapters, God has revealed himself to the world. He has clearly shown that the picture of God at the top of a high hill with various routes up to him, is absolutely wrong. It may be taught in some religious education lessons and pulpits, but it is not taught anywhere in Scripture. God, who loves so much, has leaned over backwards to show man the only way of escape from sin and to enjoy him eternally. And this way is open to all.

There are five reasons for believing that there is only one way to God.

1. God's character

There is always a tendency for man to make God in man's own image. We are small and sinful compared with the great and holy God. So many religions set rules, which they feel must be obeyed if man is ever to reach God. But, is God really that petty? If God is God, then he is infinitely greater than anything man can fully comprehend. The only hope is that God will himself stoop to reach man. If I could fully understand him, then God would not be God, and I would not be a mere mortal.

In wisdom, honour, glory and knowledge he is infinitely superior to man. He is of 'purer eyes than to behold evil and cannot look on wickedness'.[7] He is called 'Holy, holy, holy'.[8] He has never grown accustomed to sin nor trifled with it. The Ten Commandments are not only his commandments for us today, but also the expression of his character. He has never lied, stolen, been impure, coveted; he never spoke falsely.

That is why no sin will ever be allowed into heaven. On virtually the last page of the Bible we read, 'But there shall by no means enter into it anything that defiles, or causes an abomination or a lie, but only those who are written in the Lamb's book of life.'[9] Perhaps this is because, if God allowed sin into his presence, soon there would be wars and rumours of war, hatred, vice, murder and heaven would be as earth.

When John saw a vision of Jesus, we read that he 'fell at his feet as dead'.[10] Those who feel they can attain God by their own efforts have a god who is too small.

2. Man's condition

Spend too much time looking in a mirror and you may begin to wish you could not see yourself so clearly! Spend some time looking at God's honest portrayal of man in the Bible and you will see how clearly God demonstrates that all are rebels before him. In fact, God's word has accurately been described as a mirror (read James 1:22–25 and 2 Corinthians 3:18).

How honestly even the Bible's greatest characters are portrayed, 'warts and all'. Noah became a drunkard, Abraham and Sarah laughed at God's promise, Jacob deceived his own father and brother, Moses murdered, Samson squandered his strength on pagan women, David committed adultery, Solomon turned to folly, many of the kings of Israel and Judah were idolatrous, Peter denied Christ, the disciples fled and Thomas doubted him. So much for heroics! But we are all like them. 'For there is no difference; for all have sinned and fall short of the glory of God.'[11]

Good intentions, New Year's resolutions or turning

over new leaves all fail to improve our basic condition. We are plagued by sin. God's verdict on all of us is identical: 'Then the Lord saw that the wickedness of man was great in the earth, and that every intent of the thoughts of his heart was only evil continually.'[12]

It is impossible for us to lift up ourselves to God or bring God down to us. The holy God can have no dealings with sinful man. God is not sitting around a negotiating table waiting for man to raise his offer or promise obedience.

> Not the labours of my hands
> Can fulfil thy law's demands,
> Could my zeal no respite know
> Could my tears for ever flow,
> All for sin could not atone,
> Thou must save and Thou alone.[13]

The commonly-held view of Christianity that it simply teaches us to improve ourselves, or that the 'good go up and the bad go down', is far from the truth. The Bible says:

> For by grace you have been saved through faith, and that not of yourselves; it is the gift of God, not of works, lest anyone should boast.[14]

> But when the kindness and love of God our Saviour toward man appeared, not by works of righteousness which we have done, but according to his mercy he saved us, through the washing of regeneration and renewing of the Holy Spirit, whom he poured out on us absolutely through Jesus Christ our Saviour.[15]

Jesus said that he 'did not come to call [those who think they are] righteous, but sinners [who know that they are lost], to repentance'.[16]

This is not flattering to our human ego, but it is like

balm to the person who realistically sees himself not as others see him but as God sees him.

The advert showed a boy in what looked like a fine white shirt, until he compared it to a Brand X white shirt! I may be all right compared with my neighbour, but contrasted with the purity of Christ, I am guilty. But it is for such as me that he came to save.

Thomas Bilney was a young student of canon law at Oxford University in 1516. Deeply religious, he was nevertheless conscious of sin within. His priest gave the advice that he should pray and fast, but it all seemed to no avail for this devotee. Erasmus's Greek New Testament had been declared illegal by Bilney's church, but despite that he bought a copy of this new book and secretly read it. He avidly devoured the Gospels, Acts and epistles until he came to Paul's first letter to Timothy, chapter 1 verse 15: 'This is a faithful saying and worthy of all acceptance, that Christ Jesus came into the world to save sinners, of whom I am chief.' Bilney thought, 'How can Paul be the chief of sinners? I am!' Then he realised that Paul had so described himself and yet Christ had died for him, so Jesus must also have died for Thomas Bilney. Confessing nothing except his sin, Bilney claimed the forgiveness that Christ died to procure. In an instant his guilty conscience was eased and he felt inexpressible joy.

'We contribute nothing to our salvation except our sin,' said Archbishop Temple. But that is what we have most of, and Christ willingly takes it from those who give it to him.

3. Christ's claims

Tolerance is not necessarily a virtue. It depends what issue one is tolerant towards. Intolerance is not necessarily a sin. I am intolerant towards terrorists, murderers, rapists and the like. Christ, too, was deeply intolerant towards error. His harshest words were reserved not for the drunkards or immoral (though of course he deplored such wrongs), but for the religious hypocrites of the day. Christ's way is not, in fact, narrow at all; the offer of eternal life is open to all mankind, no matter what sex, age, state of health, colour, class, creed, upbringing or lifestyle.

It is ironic how those who will not submit themselves to the law of God invent other sins by which they judge society. To speak of 'a manhole' or 'blackboard' is now taboo in certain circles—they are sexist or racist terms! Meanwhile there is hardly an outcry about the flagrant denial of the Ten Commandments. Christ spoke and touched the nerve of man's sinfulness. Read for example his blistering denunciation of hypocrisy.

> The scribes and the Pharisees sit in Moses' seat. Therefore whatever they tell you to observe, that observe and do, but do not do according to their works; for they say, and do not do. For they bind heavy burdens, hard to bear, and lay them on men's shoulders; but they themselves will not move them with one of their fingers. But all their works they do to be seen by men. They make their phylacteries [boxes containing scripture verses tied to the head or arms] broad and enlarge the borders of their garments. They love the best places at feasts, the best seats in the synagogues.
>
> Woe to you, scribes and Pharisees, hypocrites! For you travel land and sea to win one proselyte, and when he is won, you make him twice as much a son of hell as yourselves.
>
> Woe to you, scribes and Pharisees, hypocrites! For you cleanse the outside of the cup and dish, but inside they are full of extortion and self-indulgence. Blind Pharisee, first cleanse the inside of the cup and dish, that the outside of them may be clean also.
>
> Woe to you scribes and Pharisees, hypocrites! For you are like whitewashed tombs which indeed appear beautiful outwardly, but inside are full of dead men's bones and all uncleanness. Even so you also outwardly appear righteous to men, but inside you are full of hypocrisy and lawlessness.

Woe to you, scribes and Pharisees, hypocrites! Because you build the tombs of the prophets and adorn the monuments of the righteous, and say, 'If we had lived in the days of our fathers, we would not have been partakers with them in the blood of the prophets.' Therefore you are witnesses against yourselves that you are sons of those who murdered the prophets.[17]

Who would feel clean enough to stand boldly before Christ's all-seeing gaze? Yet our very condition is the one which he came to deal with. He said, 'Those who are well have no need of a physician, but those who are sick.'[18] His express mission on earth was to die so that he could be the means whereby God could forgive sins. He was born to do just that. It is the work of God, and an evidence that Christ is himself God, that he could eradicate the guilty part of ordinary men and women.

If nobody is good enough for God, or able to climb up to him, then our only hope is that he would come down to us, to forgive the sin and remove the barrier that separates us from him. That is exactly what Christ has done.

He set his face steadfastly to go to Jerusalem where he would die, bearing in his own body the sin of us all.

All we like sheep have gone astray; we have turned, every one, to his own way; and the Lord has laid on him the iniquity of us all.[19]

For Christ also suffered once for sins, the just for the unjust, that he might bring us to God, being put to death in the flesh but made alive by the Spirit.[20]

Who himself bore our sins in his own body on the tree, that we, having died to sins, might live for righteousness—by whose stripes you were healed.[21]

But God demonstrates his own love towards us, in that while we were still sinners, Christ died for us.[22]

Imagine a person drowning at sea. Standing on the seashore are people like Buddha, Mohammed, Moses, the gurus and a host of other religious leaders. All are shouting instructions to the desperate man. Each tells him how to swim. Each piece of advice is contradicting the others. In contrast, Jesus dives in to rescue the man. In so doing, Christ gives his own life.

In reality this is the difference between Christianity and other religions. Far from man striving to reach God, Christ came to rescue us. We need to trust, not try. Instead of 'being' and 'doing', we should rely on who Christ is and what he has done.

That is why Christ could say, 'I am the way, the truth, and the life. No one comes to the Father except through me';[23] and: 'I am the door. If anyone enters by me, he will be saved, and will go in and out and find pasture.'[24]

These are not the words of a mere prophet, or we would accuse Christ of megalomania or delusion. There is an exclusiveness about Christ, or as someone put it, 'If all religions are right, then Jesus is right, and if Jesus is right, then all other religions are wrong. Right?!' Christ is the only way to God, because he came from God to remove all that cuts us off and keeps us from God.

Peter, the apostle and early preacher, claimed, 'Nor is there salvation in any other, for there is no other name under heaven given among men by which we must be saved.'[25]

Paul wrote, 'For there is one God and one mediator between God and men, the man Christ Jesus.'[26]

In Athens at the famous 'Speakers' Corner' called the Areopagus, Paul said:

> Truly, these times of ignorance God overlooked, but now commands all men everywhere to repent, because he has appointed a day on which he will judge the world in righteousness by the man whom he has ordained. He has given assurance of this to all, by raising him from the dead.[27]

Christ is not an option to be selected or rejected, but the only way to God, the one who should be received as Saviour and Lord. If there were any other means whereby sin could be forgiven, God would not have allowed Jesus to die so brutally under the crushing load of sin.

If Christ were anything less than God manifest in the flesh, then God would not have raised him from the dead. R. A. Torrey said:

> When Jesus died, he died as my representative, and I died in him; when he arose, he rose as my representative, and I arose in him; when he ascended up on high and took his place at the right hand of the Father in the glory, he ascended as my representative and I ascended in him, and today I am seated in Christ with God in the heavenlies. I look at the cross of Christ, and I know that atonement has been made for my sins; I look at the open sepulchre and the risen and ascended Lord, and I know the atonement has been accepted. There no longer remains a single sin on me, no matter how many or how great my sins may have been.[28]

The Bible says, Jesus 'was delivered up because of our offences, and raised because of our justification'.[29]

For three days as Jesus' body lay in the tomb, a watching and waiting mankind could have wondered if Christ's death was sufficient to atone for the sins of the world. When Jesus rose and the stone rolled away from the tomb, no-one needed to doubt. Christ was risen; God could now reign in the hearts of those who would believe on him.

It is possible to visit the tombs of many influential world leaders, both political and religious. All die. Only Christ's tomb is empty. Only he rose from the dead. This is the great sign that he is reliable. In fact the Jews asked Jesus what sign did he give since he claimed God was his Father: 'Jesus answered and said to them, "Destroy this temple, and in three days I will raise it up."...But he was speaking of the temple of his body.'[30]

On another occasion Jesus said:

> No sign will be given [to this generation] except... As Jonah was three days and three nights in the belly of the great fish, so will the Son of Man be three days and three nights in the heart of the earth.[31]

God is willing to reckon and declare men righteous on the basis of Christ's death and resurrection for them. No other way has ever been provided.

4. The gospel's call

The cross of Christ as the means for man to be brought back into fellowship with God was not an afterthought of God. It is, in fact, the theme of the Old and New Testaments.

Christ's death was anticipated

As soon as Adam and Eve had sinned, God made a specific promise. To the serpent God spoke: 'I will put enmity between you and the woman, and between your seed and her seed. He shall bruise your head, and you shall bruise his heel.'[32]

Note that only the seed of *the woman* is mentioned. So early in the Scriptures there is a prophecy of the virgin birth. Indeed, Christ bruised the head of the serpent Satan as he conquered the great weapons of sin and death by dying and rising again.

Seven hundred years before Jesus' birth, Isaiah the prophet wrote:

> He is despised and rejected by men, a man of sorrows and acquainted with grief. And we hid, as it were, our faces from him; he was despised, and we did not esteem him. Surely he has borne our griefs and carried our sorrows; yet

we esteemed him stricken, smitten by God, and afflicted. But he was wounded for our transgressions, he was bruised for our iniquities; the chastisement for our peace was upon him, and by his stripes we are healed. All we like sheep have gone astray; we have turned, every one, to his own way; and the Lord has laid on him the iniquity of us all. He was oppressed and he was afflicted, yet he opened not his mouth; he was led as a lamb to the slaughter, and as a sheep before its shearers is silent, so he opened not his mouth. He was taken from prison and from judgment, and who will declare his generation? For he was cut off from the land of the living; for the transgressions of my people he was stricken. And they made his grave with the wicked—but with the rich at his death, because he had done no violence, nor was any deceit in his mouth.[33]

Earlier, David in the Psalms had written prophetically the words and work of Christ as he suffered as a servant atoning for sin.

My God, my God, why have you forsaken me?...All those who see me laugh me to scorn; they shoot out the lip, they shake the head, saying, 'He trusted in the Lord, let him rescue him; let him deliver him, since he delights in him!' I am poured out like water, and all my bones are out of joint; my heart is like wax; it has melted within me.[34]

Not only through prophecy, but also pictures, every obedient Israelite who lived before Messiah (or Christ) came eagerly anticipated his coming. Conscious of guilt, a Jew would take a spotless male lamb to the priest, who would lay his hand, along with that of the sinner, on the head of the lamb. Then the lamb would die as its blood was shed as a sacrifice and substitute for sin. Every time this ritual was performed it was a shadowy prefiguring of Christ dying as 'The Lamb of God who takes away the sin of the world!'[35] Jesus was to die as the sacrifice and substitute for our sin.

At the time of Jesus' birth, the angel said to Joseph,

'You shall call his name Jesus, for he will save his people from their sins.'[36] The very name Jesus means 'Saviour'.

Then Christ himself anticipated his own death. He said repeatedly, 'My hour has not yet come',[37] until the time of his crucifixion when he said, 'The hour has come.'[38] Jesus said, 'For even the Son of Man did not come to be served, but to serve, and to give his life a ransom for many' and, 'The Son of Man is about to be betrayed into the hands of men, and they will kill him and the third day he will be raised up.'[39]

Even in the great moment of glory when Jesus was transfigured we read that Christ spoke about the death that he was about to bring to fulfilment in Jerusalem.[40]

Jesus asked his disciples: 'Who do men say that I, the Son of Man, am?' Apparently there were various rumours, some thinking that he was John the Baptist, Elijah, Jeremiah or one of the prophets. When asked, 'But who do you say that I am?' Peter answered resoundingly, 'You are the Christ, the Son of the living God.'[41] As the disciples clearly understood who the man was, Jesus immediately explained his mission, so we read: 'From that time Jesus began to show to his disciples that he must go to Jerusalem, and suffer many things from the elders and chief priests and scribes, and be killed, and be raised again the third day.'[42]

Later Jesus warned again of all that would happen: 'The Son of Man is about to be betrayed into the hands of men, and they will kill him, and the third day he will be raised up.'[43]

Christ was not caught unawares or taken by surprise when he was betrayed, arrested, manhandled and crucified. As soon as man had sinned, God had revealed his plan and given his promise. Thousands of years later as man did his worst, God gave his best and fulfilled the anticipation of the ages.

Christ's death was accomplished

When Jesus cried, 'It is finished,'[44] this was not the defeated moan of a dying man, but the victorious cry of Christ's completed work. The Greek word used here actually means 'completely complete' or 'perfectly perfect'.

Many things in this world are not finished. We have an 'unfinished symphony', plans, books, architecture and dreams. Jesus at the age of thirty-three finished the work he was born to do.

F. W. Farrar, in his book *The Life of Christ*,[45] describes the awful physical trauma of execution by crucifixion:

> For indeed a death by crucifixion seems to include all that pain and death can have of horrible and ghastly—dizziness, cramp, thirst, starvation, sleeplessness, traumatic fever, tetanus, shame, publicity of shame, long continuance of torment, horror of anticipation, mortification of untended wounds—all intensified just up to the point at which they can be endured at all, but all stopping just short of the point which would give to the sufferer the relief of unconsciousness.
>
> The unnatural position made every movement painful; the lacerated veins and crushed tendons throbbed with incessant anguish; the wounds, inflamed by exposure, gradually gangrened; the arteries—especially at the head and stomach—became swollen and oppressed with surcharged blood; and while each variety of misery went on gradually increasing, there was added to them the intolerable pang of a burning and raging thirst; and all these physical complications caused an internal excitement and anxiety, which made the prospect of death itself—of death, the unknown enemy, at whose approach man usually shudders most—bear the aspect of a delicious and exquisite release.

Man did his worst against Jesus. So did God: 'It was

the Lord's will to crush him and cause him to suffer...the Lord makes his life a guilt offering.'[46]

God laid on him the weight of the world's sin. The vile deeds that hit the headlines as well as the everyday sins of us all were compacted on to the pure, holy, undefiled Jesus. Like a railway guard's van with its brakes applied, standing still as the weight of all the goods wagons are shunted on to it, so Christ stood under the crushing load of the sin of the world. He paid the price of every last wrong thought, word and deed, past, present and future. Sins of wrong attitudes and actions, of omission and commission, of things remembered by us or forgotten, were all on Christ. He was actually, 'smitten by God, and afflicted'[47] At this point came the *coup de grâce*. Even worse than the bearing of all that sin was the inevitable consequence of it—for the first time in his life, Jesus was cut off from his Father because our sin, which he was carrying in our place, cut him off. Our sin separated him from his Father and caused God's face to be hidden. The grief this caused Christ was expressed in his agonising cry from the cross: 'My God, my God, why have you forsaken me?'[48]

Yet all this was in fulfilment of the plan of the loving triune God: 'For God so loved the world that he gave his only begotten Son, that whoever believes in him should not perish but have everlasting life.'[49]

Christ's death must be appropriated

God's greatest offer to each individual is that he will forgive any who come to him. God is not in a hurry to judge, though judge he must. The door of Noah's ark remained open seven days as an act of invitation to all to enter. Then God finally closed the door. The Israelites marched for seven days around the walls of Jericho before they eventually fell. In contrast, the prodigal son's father in Jesus' parable ran to meet and greet his returning child. It is all a picture of a God who is slow to judge but in a hurry to save those who will turn in repentance and faith to him, a God who is patient, 'not willing that any should perish but that all should come to repentance.'[50]

Martin Luther, the great German reformer, received a letter from a distressed monk. In his reply Luther wrote:

> Learn to know Christ and him crucified. Learn to sing to him and say, 'Lord Jesus, you are my righteousness, I am your sin; you took on you what was mine, yet set on me what was yours. You became what you were not, that I might become what I was not.[51]

That is it. Christ's work can be appropriated by an act of faith, a decision to believe. When a couple stand at the front of a church and make vows committing themselves to each other in marriage, their words change their whole status before God, each other and society. So, too, if we will receive Christ, words that confess sin and express our trust in his finished work need to be framed in the mind or spoken audibly as the expression of an enduring commitment.

Even now, you could ask Christ to be your personal Saviour and Lord.

5. The Christian's certainty

I have asked many a person if they are sure of going to heaven when they die. Usually their hope is based on the false view that their deeds are good enough to grant them a place in heaven, forgetting that God sees into the secret recesses of all our minds and lives.[52] Jesus warned all such when, in the Sermon on the Mount, he said:

> Not everyone who says to me, 'Lord, Lord,' shall enter the kingdom of heaven, but he who does the will of my Father in heaven. Many will say to me in that day, 'Lord, Lord,

have we not prophesied in your name, cast our demons in your name, and done many wonders in your name?' And then I will declare to them, 'I never knew you; depart from me, you who practise lawlessness!'[53]

In contrast, Christians know for sure that instead of the hell they deserve they are guaranteed heaven as a free gift from a loving God.

Look at some of these promises in the Bible, which speak of the Christian's certainty:

He who believes in the Son has everlasting life; and he who does not believe the Son shall not see life, but the wrath of God abides on him.[54]

Most assuredly, I say to you, he who hears my word and believes in him who sent me has everlasting life, and shall not come into judgment, but has passed from death into life.[55]

Most assuredly, I say to you, he who believes in me has everlasting life.[56]

These things I have written to you who believe in the name of the Son of God, that you may know that you have eternal life, and that you may continue to believe in the name of the Son of God.[57]

Therefore we are always confident, knowing that while we are at home in the body we are absent from the Lord. We are confident, yes, well pleased rather to be absent from the body and to be present with the Lord.[58]

For our citizenship is in heaven, from which we also eagerly wait for the Saviour, the Lord Jesus Christ.[59]

That if you confess with your mouth the Lord Jesus and believe in your heart that God has raised him from the dead,

you will be saved. For with the heart one believes to righteousness, and with the mouth confession is made to salvation. For the Scripture says, 'Whoever believes on him will
not be put to shame.' For 'whoever calls upon the name of
the Lord shall be saved.'[60]

Christian experience is not 'pie in the sky when you
die!' but rather steak on the plate while you wait!

A Christian actually knows God in the here and now.
He is real to every believer. Christ has become a friend
and very present help to the Christian. 'He who did not
spare his own Son, but delivered him up for us all'[61] also
gives us all the things we need.

It is a wonderful experience to know that 'there is now
no condemnation' because we are 'in Christ Jesus'.[62]
Christ has dealt with the Christian's past, he is dealing
with his present and he guarantees his future.

This very moment, will you trust Christ as your Saviour and Lord and as the one who will reconcile you to
God for ever?

Notes

1. Billy Graham, *Calling Youth to Christ*.
2. Genesis 4.
3. Romans 10:2,3.
4. Romans 5:8.
5. Matthew 5:43–47.
6. Matthew 25:31–46.
7. Habakkuk 1:13.
8. Isaiah 6:3; Revelation 4:8.
9. Revelation 21:27.
10. Revelation 1:17.
11. Romans 3:22,23.
12. Genesis 6:5.
13. A. Toplady (from the hymn *Rock of Ages*).
14. Ephesians 2:8,9.
15. Titus 3:4–6.

16. Matthew 9:13.
17. Matthew 23:2–6,15,25–31.
18. Matthew 9:12.
19. Isaiah 53:6.
20. 1 Peter 3:18.
21. 1 Peter 2:24.
22. Romans 5:8.
23. John 14:6.
24. John 10:9.
25. Acts 4:12.
26. 1 Timothy 2:5.
27. Acts 17:30–31.
28. R.A. Torrey, *The Bible and its Christ* (Fleming H. Revell, New Jersey: Old Tappan, n.d., pp.107,108).
29. Romans 4:25.
30. John 2:18–22.
31. Matthew 12:39,40.
32. Genesis 3:15.
33. Isaiah 53:3–9.
34. Psalm 22:1,7,8,14.
35. John 1:29.
36. Matthew 1:21.
37. John 2:4.
38. John 17:1.
39. Mark 10:45; Matthew 17:22.
40. See Luke 9:31.
41. See Matthew 16:13–16.
42. Matthew 16:21.
43. Matthew 17:22,23.
44. John 19:30.
45. *The Life of Christ* (Dutton, Dovar, Cassell & Co., 1897, p.440).
46. Isaiah 53:10, New International Version.
47. Isaiah 53:4.
48. Matthew 27:46; Mark 15:34.
49. John 3:16.
50. 2 Peter 3:9.
51. Theodore G. Tappert (ed.), *The Library of Christian Classics*, Vol XVIII (CSM, 1955, p.110: 'Letters of Spiritual Counsel').
52. 1 Samuel 16:7.

53. Matthew 7:21–23.
54. John 3:36.
55. John 5:24.
56. John 6:47.
57. 1 John 5:13.
58. 2 Corinthians 5:6,8.
59. Philippians 3:20.
60. Romans 10:9–11,13.
61. Romans 8:32.
62. Romans 8:1.

8

Will You Believe?

Jesus said: *You must be born again.... Unless one is born again, he cannot see the kingdom of God.*
John 3:7,3

Today, if you will hear his voice, do not harden your hearts.
Hebrews 3:7

Having sought to explain various aspects of the Christian gospel, as well as briefly looking at a tiny tip of the iceberg of evidence, what will you do about Christ?

The claims of Christ are such that they demand a response. The Bible asks, 'How long will you falter between two opinions? If the Lord is God, follow him; but if Baal, then follow him.'[1] Baal was a pagan god, symbolising all that comes between us and the living God. We read, 'Choose for yourselves this day whom you will serve.'[2]

The most important task in life is to make sure that you are at peace with God. God's word, the Bible, tells us how this is possible, and why it is necessary.

Below is a straightforward summary of the Bible's teaching about how you may find peace with God and become at one with him. If you can go along with each step, then I suggest you pray a prayer similar to the one at the end of the chapter as an act of repentance and faith.

We read in the Bible: 'But as many as received him, to them he gave the right to become children of God, even to those who believe in his name.'[3]

We must receive Christ first as our Sin-bearer

We have seen that when the Lord Jesus died on the cross, God laid all our sins on him. Therefore we need to receive Christ as Sin-bearer. We must confess to God (that is, agree with him) that we are guilty of sin, make a positive decision to turn away from that sin, and ask him to pardon us. The Bible says:

> All we like sheep have gone astray; we have turned, every one, to his own way; and the Lord has laid on him the iniquity of us all.[4]

> Who himself bore our sins in his own body on the tree.[5]

Secondly, we must receive Christ as our Saviour

The Lord Jesus not only died; he also rose from the dead. As Saviour, Jesus both forgives past sin and gives us strength to live a new life. Asking him into our lives means taking him as the one who will give us power over sin day by day. The Holy Spirit (God himself) will live within us. The Bible says:

> Therefore he is also able to save to the uttermost those who come to God through him, since he ever lives to make intercession for them.[6]

> For in that he himself has suffered, being tempted, he is able to aid those who are tempted.[7]

> Or do you not know that your body is the temple of the Holy Spirit who is in you, whom you have from God, and you are not your own? For you were bought at a price; therefore glorify God in your body and in your spirit, which are God's.[8]

Thirdly, we must receive Christ as our Sovereign

Trusting the Lord Jesus is not only asking him to cleanse the past, but also to take charge of the present and the future. He will guide our lives as we serve and obey him in everything. The Bible says:

> For to this end Christ died and rose and lived again, that he might be Lord of both the dead and the living.[9]

> Jesus said: 'If anyone desires to come after me, let him deny himself, and take up his cross daily, and follow me.'[10]

> God...now commands all men everywhere to repent and believe.[11]

This means we must be willing to turn from sin and turn in complete trust to Christ. As we do, God turns to us—he works a miracle in us.

Will you now pray, asking the Lord Jesus to be your personal Sin-bearer, Saviour and Sovereign? In the moment that you sincerely trust Christ, he will forgive you and make you his for ever. The Bible says:

> The one who comes to me, I will by no means cast out.[12]

> And I give them eternal life, and they shall never perish; neither shall anyone snatch them out of my hand.[13]

> These things I have written to you who believe...that you may know that you have eternal life.[14]

Many have found that praying with similar words to the ones below has helped them in the act of putting their trust in Christ. Will you pray like this now?

Heavenly Father, I confess my sin to you and want to repent of it. Please forgive me. I trust Christ as my

Sin-bearer, my Saviour and my Sovereign. Help me grow to become a strong Christian. Thank you for loving me. I pray in Jesus' name. Amen.

If you have prayed this and, as far as you are able, have meant what you have said, then you are a new creation in Christ, you have been born again of the Spirit! It will be helpful to write down the date you prayed like this, and to tell someone of your new found faith and life in Christ. He has promised abundant life from now on, life with purpose, direction and meaning.

This is the first day of a new life...

Notes

1. 1 Kings 18:21.
2. Joshua 24:15.
3. John 1:12.
4. Isaiah 53:6.
5. 1 Peter 2:24.
6. Hebrews 7:25.
7. Hebrews 2:18.
8. 1 Corinthians 6:19,20.
9. Romans 14:9.
10. Luke 9:23.
11. Acts 17:30.
12. John 6:37.
13. John 10:28.
14. 1 John 5:13.

9

When You Believe

Therefore, if anyone is in Christ, he is a new creation; old things have passed away; behold, all things have become new.
2 Corinthians 5:17

If you have prayed the prayer at the end of chapter 8 and meant it and, as far as you can tell, have genuinely repented and believed in Christ, then you will want to start to live for him who has promised his new life in you. The Lord wants us to be holy, because he is holy,[1] and he doesn't ask us to do anything without revealing the way and providing the means. We read, 'His divine power has given to us all things that pertain to life and godliness, through the knowledge of him who called us by glory and virtue.'[2] Jesus never promised that the Christian life would be easy. As we saw earlier, Jesus said, 'If anyone desires to come after me, let him deny himself, and take up his cross daily, and follow me';[3] and Paul knew that 'all who desire to live godly in Christ Jesus will suffer persecution.[4] However, there is a wonderful joy and peace that can be experienced only by the Christian.

> Trust and obey,
> For there's no other way
> To be happy in Jesus,
> But to trust and obey.[5]

Christian living is an adventure in which God wants

your joy to be full and your steps to be directed by his loving hand. Peter said that when we believe in him we are filled with an inexpressible and glorious joy.[6]

Christianity is not a club, hobby, or sideline. It is a lifelong developing relationship with the loving God whose desire is towards the individual believer. He wants to mould and make the Christian into somebody who is Christlike.[7] It is his desire that every believer in Christ will become ever more like him, exhibiting the fruit of the Holy Spirit in their lives: love, joy, peace, long-suffering, kindness, goodness, faithfulness, gentleness and self-control.[8] One day, he will take home each one who is trusting in Christ alone for salvation, to be with him in heaven. Before that time, if you are a Christian, you have the privilege of serving him who saved you. A vital first step in this service is baptism.

Baptism

We saw in the preceding chapter that a personal response is required of each of us as we come face to face with Christ. Having responded by believing, trusting in and following Christ, the next step in your new life is the response of baptism. This is a symbolic sharing in the death, burial and resurrection of Jesus, as explained by Paul in the book of Romans, chapter 6. It is done publicly as a profession of faith in Christ and all that he has done for us. It is the badge of Christian discipleship. If you read the book of Acts you will find many instances of people repenting, believing in Christ and being baptised.[9] Baptism is a vital step in your Christian life, not least because it is done in obedience to Christ's own command.[10] The Bible tells us that by hearing and obeying the Lord, we build our lives on the Rock[11] and are progressively made more and more like Christ himself.[12] Obedience then is God's pathway for the Christian in his desire to 'be holy'; the means is the Holy Spirit, our helper and comforter, the one who comes alongside us to guide us and help us understand what God has freely given us.[13]

Here now are some suggestions, that I would heartily commend to you as a new believer.

1. Give God the first day of every week

Under increasing attack as it is, in Western countries we still have a heritage wherein Sunday, the first day of the week,[14] is set apart as God's day. The Jews kept Saturday as their Sabbath to remind them of the work of the Father in creation. God rested in triumph on the seventh day of creation. We keep Sunday as 'the Lord's day',[15] which reminds us not only of the work of the Father in *creation*, but also of the work of the Son in *recreation* (he rose from the dead on the Sunday morning) and the work of the Holy Spirit in *procreation* (he came upon the gathered Christians, seven weeks later at Pentecost). There are jobs that have to be done every day of the week, including Sunday. The Lord Jesus spoke about works of mercy or necessity and, of course, there will be Christians involved in these. However, every Christian needs the company of other Christians so that together they can worship, work and witness to the Lord.

Find a church: (i) that believes the Bible; (ii) that preaches the atoning blood of Christ; (iii) where you can meet with brothers and sisters in Christ; and (iv) where you can take others for whom you are praying. No church is perfect; after all, Christians are simply forgiven sinners. But a church is not really a church if 'another gospel' is preached, which does not focus attention on 'Jesus Christ and him crucified.'[16] Look up and read Galatians chapter 1, verses 8 and 9.

As you go to church with others you will learn more about God and how to worship him. Take notes from the sermons. If there is anything you don't understand, ask questions and start to become familiar with the Bible.

D.L. Moody, the evangelist, said: 'Carry your Bible to church and you will preach a sermon a mile long!'[17] If you are able, as soon as you can, start to attend the mid-week Bible study and prayer meeting and get involved in working for the cause of Christ. There are many churches praying that God will send them godly workers. However, you should not feel that you have to get involved with every church project in order to be accepted by God or the church. Nor need you feel condemned if you cannot attend all meetings. The Lord himself is your priority, and you probably have family responsibilities too.

Sunday afternoon and evening can be a time of reading for spiritual growth. Reading is to the mind what eating is to the body. Reading good Christian biography feeds the mind, fills the heart and fires the spirit. It is often the antidote to lethargic living and dull conversation. Although not inspired in the same way as Scripture, many a Christian has found the right biography to be spiritually uplifting. God has used books as the instrument to call the believer into sacrificial unstinting service. The following books I would consider as investments for life. They are the beginner's basic diet and the mature Christian's reminder of the kind of life to which we are called. It may take a few years to get through them all, but biography has been used of God to keep Christians spiritually sharp.

I therefore recommend them to you. Sell your coat to buy them! Set aside time to read them:

1. *Biography of James Hudson Taylor*, Dr & Mrs Howard Taylor (1973), Hodder & Stoughton.
2. *Autobiography of C.H. Spurgeon*: Volume One, *The Early Years* (1967) and Volume Two, *The Full Harvest* (1973), Banner of Truth.
3. *George Müller: Delighted in God*, Roger Steer (revised 1990), Hodder & Stoughton. (The classic,

George Müller of Bristol by A.T. Pierson (1972), is
no longer in print.)
4. *Five English Reformers*, J.C. Ryle (1960), Banner
of Truth.
5. *Journal of John Wesley*, edited by Christopher Idle
(1986), Lion Publishing.
6. *Robert Murray McCheyne: Memoirs and Remains*,
Andrew Bonar (1966), Banner of Truth.
7. *The Life and Diary of David Brainerd*, Jonathan
Edwards, ed. (1989), Baker Book House.
8. *Through Gates of Splendour*, Elizabeth Elliot
(revised 1988), STL Books.
9. *Great Christians You Should Know*, Warren
Wiersbe (1986), Inter-Varsity Press.

You will soon find that Christians, despite all their
failings, can become the finest friends in the world.
Christians are great fun to be with for, after all, they are
at peace with God and enjoy his peace in their hearts.
However, don't just fritter away time with them, but talk
of spiritual things and seek to serve God together.

The Bible makes mention of the phrase 'one another'
many times. It says, for example, that Christians should:

Love one another—John 13:34
Bear with one another—Ephesians 4:2
Be kind to one another—Ephesians 4:32
Forgive one another—Ephesians 4:32
Comfort one another—1 Thessalonians 4:18
Consider one another—Hebrews 10:24
Pray for one another—James 5:16
Show compassion to one another—1 Peter 3:8
Be hospitable to one another—1 Peter 4:9

Often the zeal and joy of a new convert can be a rich
blessing and challenge to those who have been Christians

for some years. 'Not forsaking the assembling of ourselves together...but exhorting one another,'[18] says the
Bible.

2. Give God the first minutes of every day

Never neglect daily Bible reading and private prayer.
Ideally it is best to give God the first few minutes of our
day. But, of course, he knows that this is not always
possible due to some people's circumstances. Such
people will want to find another part of the day, which is
more appropriate. However, it is important that you do
set aside a specific time for just you and the Lord. The
Bible is the major way that God has revealed to us his
character and his will. His word is living and powerful[19]
and through it God will speak to you. The more you get
to know him, the more you will love him and want to
spend time with him. Prayer is equally vital in drawing
close to God. Prayer is, in essence, communion with
God: you speaking with him and he with you. God will
speak to you principally through the Bible and you will
speak to God through prayer. The Bible and prayer are
vital for the Christian life. The Bible will keep you from
sin, or sin will keep you from the Bible.

As well as reading some verses every day, it is good to
study the Scriptures systematically. I would recommend
reading through the New Testament chapter by chapter
first of all. You could then read the Old and New Testaments together, perhaps a few chapters of each every
day. 'As newborn babes, desire the pure milk of the
word, that you may grow thereby.'[20]

Underline verses that 'speak' to you and write down
thoughts that come to mind as you read. Memorise key
Bible verses. David knew the value of this discipline:
'Your word I have hidden in my heart, that I might not
sin against you.'[21] Also pass on verses to others—after
all, expression deepens impression! Unless you become

a man or woman of the Bible, you may be tossed around by new winds of doctrine, which come and go so quickly.

Archbishop Usher said, 'My greatest delight in life is to be in a nook with the Book!' If you can get into the daily dogged discipline of Bible reading, you will find it becomes a delight.

When I was converted at the age of fifteen in the Lebanon, the man who led me to Christ, the Reverend Hagop Sagharian, said, 'Make an appointment to meet with God at a particular time and place, and never keep God waiting!' It was good advice. Hudson Taylor said, 'A man may be dedicated and devoted but if ill-disciplined, he will be useless.'

Don't necessarily expect verses and thoughts to jump out at you, but as you pray and read your Bible God will teach you truths that will leave abiding and life-transforming impressions on you.

All relationships involve two-way communication. Turn the things you have read into prayer. All that you read in the Bible seek to obey. Pray and ask God to help, and then simply do what God says.

In prayer thank God for all he has done and praise him for who he is. Pray for your family, friends, church and nation, as well as your own needs. God hears and delights to answer prayer. Jesus said:

> Ask, and it will be given to you; seek, and you will find; knock, and it will be opened to you. For everyone who asks receives, and he who seeks finds, and to him who knocks it will be opened. Or what man is there among you who, if his son asks for bread, will give him a stone? Or if he asks for a fish, will he give him a serpent? If you then, being evil, know how to give good gifts to your children, how much more will your Father who is in heaven give good things to those who ask him![22]

If you note down your prayer requests, you will soon find that God is answering prayer, not always in the way that you would imagine, but always for your good and his glory.

When you do sin, confess it to God at once, then believe it is forgiven, because God says so. A child who is naughty, whether deliberately or unintentionally, does not cease to be the child of his father because of his misdemeanour. Likewise, you have not lost your position as a child of God, but until there is confession and forgiveness, you have lost your close fellowship with him; sin always causes separation. The Bible says: 'If we confess our sins, he is faithful and just to forgive us our sins and to cleanse us from all unrighteousness.'[23]

However, this is not an excuse for us to sin. The Bible also warns that: 'Whatever a man sows, that he will also reap. For he who sows to his flesh will of the flesh reap corruption, but he who sows to the Spirit will of the Spirit reap everlasting life.'[24] J.C. Ryle said, 'Never expect sin, never excite sin and never excuse sin.' Though sin may be forgiven, consequences and scars may remain.

This daily 'quiet time', or 'meeting with God', will become the highlight of your day as you do business with him. There is no substitute for time spent with the Lord.

3. Give God the first portion of all you have

Giving to God involves not just our finances but our possessions, our time and our talents; in fact, all that we are and have. Christ, the King of glory who was rich in heaven, became poor for us.[25] He was born in a borrowed manger, preached from a borrowed boat, rode to Jerusalem on a borrowed donkey, borrowed a coin to make a point about allegiances, and was buried in a tomb that was not his own. He said, 'Foxes have holes and birds of the air have nests, but the Son of Man has nowhere to lay his head.'[26] He set an example of sacrifice for those he loved. Nobody will compel you or check up on your giving as a Christian. However, there is great joy

in being able to meet the needs of others through all that
God has given to us. Jesus said, 'It is more blessed to
give than receive.'[27] We should do this systematically,
sacrificially, and cheerfully. What is more, the Lord has
promised that when we give to his work in this way, he
will throw open 'the windows of heaven and pour out
[for us] so much blessing that there will not be room
enough to receive it'![28]

There are great needs in the world. It is vital that all
hear the good news that Christ Jesus came into the world
to save sinners. We should do everything we can to help
in the great cause of spreading the gospel, the commission that Christ gave to all disciples.[29] To give you vision
for what the Lord is doing in other parts of the world you
could start regularly to read a missionary magazine and
pray for the work of God overseas, though never forgetting that wherever you are right now you are surrounded
by needy, hurting people. In certain countries Christians
are suffering for their faith. We can help to support
them, practically as well as by praying. And always keep
your ear tuned to the Holy Spirit's prompting—he may
call you to go yourself!

Christians have always sought to follow Christ's example of caring for the sick and underprivileged. So many
of the great social reformers, as well as hospital, school
and orphanage founders, have been Christians. As
believers we are to love God and our neighbours;[30] this
is the royal law or the law of liberty as the Bible calls it.[31]
To be involved in the work that God will direct us to,
work that springs from our faith in Christ,[32] is part of our
Christian service.

4. Give God the first consideration in every decision

God will guide you in all the decisions you have to make
if you pray, obey his word and wait for his perfect
timing. He will never lead you against what he has
already expressly commanded in the Bible.

In your prayers, humbly remind God of these promises in his word and ask him to lead you:

I will instruct you and teach you in the way you should go.[33]

Trust in the Lord with all your heart, and lean not on your own understanding; in all your ways acknowledge him, and he shall direct your paths.[34]

The Lord will guide you continually, and satisfy your soul in drought, and strengthen your bones; you shall be like a watered garden, and like a spring of water, whose waters do not fail.[35]

If any of you lacks wisdom, let him ask of God, who gives to all liberally and without reproach, and it will be given to him. But let him ask in faith, with no doubting, for he who doubts is like a wave of the sea driven and tossed by the wind.[36]

If ever you are in doubt as to whether something is right or wrong, ask these three questions:

i. Will it hinder the growth of my spiritual life? The Bible says: 'Let us lay aside every weight and the sin which so easily ensnares.'[37]

ii. Could it influence someone else in the wrong direction? The Bible says: 'Beware lest somehow this liberty of yours should become a stumbling-block to those who are weak.'[38]

iii. Will it displease my Master? The Bible says: 'Therefore, whether you eat or drink, or whatever you do, do all to the glory of God.'[39]

Pray about it and God will show you what to do. If you are still in doubt, hold back. We are to aim to be as holy as it is possible to be this side of eternity.

5. Give God the first place in your heart

The Christian is the dwelling place of God himself. Whereas he once came among his people in a tabernacle and later a temple built with hands, now he dwells within each individual believer by his Holy Spirit:

> Or do you not know that your body is the temple of the Holy Spirit who is in you, whom you have from God, and you are not your own? For you were bought at a price; therefore glorify God in your body and in your spirit, which are God's.[40]

We read: 'For by one Spirit we were all baptised into one body...and have all been made to drink into one Spirit.'[41]

Because we are his and he is ours, we are 'complete in him'.[42] Every Christian should pray that Christ 'in all things may have the pre-eminence'.[43]

The Holy Spirit living within is like floodlights on a football pitch, taking the attention from them on to someone else. The Holy Spirit makes much of Christ.[44]

Share the gospel with others by the things you say and the way you live. Never be a secret disciple, but make it your constant aim to introduce others to Christ.

The Bible says: 'But sanctify the Lord God in your hearts, and always be ready to give a defence to everyone who asks you a reason for the hope that is in you, with meekness and fear. But do this with gentleness and respect.'[45]

Jesus said: 'Therefore whoever confesses me before men, him I will also confess before my Father who is in heaven,[46] and, 'Go into all the world and preach the gospel to every creature.'[47]

Jesus will make you a 'fisher of men' if you follow him.[48]

Don't allow sin, slothfulness or side-tracks to distract you from the centrality of Christ. Keep trusting the Lord Jesus, your living Saviour, in every moment of doubt, temptation or difficulty. He is your constant companion. Ask him and he will take you through every situation. The Bible says:

Casting all your care upon him, for he cares for you.[49]

Fear not, for I am with you; be not dismayed, for I am your God. I will strengthen you, yes, I will help you, I will uphold you with my righteous right hand.[50]

You can never out-give him who has given his all for us. 'He honours those who honour him.'[51] He will meet your every need, be it of the body, soul or spirit, material, temporal or eternal.

If you are tempted to doubt, remind yourself of God's precious promises to be found throughout the Bible, and how every one is 'yes' in Christ.[52]

In triumph and jubilation Paul wrote:

Who shall separate us from the love of Christ? Shall tribulation, or distress, or persecution, or famine, or nakedness, or peril, or sword? As it is written: 'For your sake we are killed all day long; we are accounted as sheep for the slaughter.' Yet in all these things we are more than conquerors through him who loved us. For I am persuaded that neither death nor life, nor angels nor principalities nor powers, nor things present nor things to come, nor height nor depth, nor any other created thing, shall be able to separate us from the love of God which is in Christ Jesus our Lord.[53]

Notes

1. 1 Peter 1:16.
2. 2 Peter 1:3.
3. Luke 9:23.
4. 2 Timothy 3:12.
5. John Henry Sammis (from the hymn *When We Walk with the Lord*).
6. 1 Peter 1:8.
7. Romans 8:29.
8. Galatians 5:22,23.
9. Acts 2:38,41; 8:12,13,36–38; 9:18; 10:47,48; 16:31–34; 18:8.

10. Matthew 28:19.
11. Matthew 7:24.
12. John 17:17; 1 Peter 1:22.
13. 1 Corinthians 2:12.
14. Matthew 28:1; Acts 20:7; 1 Corinthians 16:2.
15. Revelation 1:10.
16. 1 Corinthians 2:2.
17. If you need to buy a Bible, I particularly recommend for its reliability and readability The New King James Version (or, as it is sometimes described, The Revised Authorised Version).
18. Hebrews 10:25.
19. Hebrews 4:12.
20. 1 Peter 2:2.
21. Psalm 119:11.
22. Matthew 7:7–11.
23. 1 John 1:9.
24. Galatians 6:7,8.
25. 2 Corinthians 8:9.
26. Luke 9:58.
27. Acts 20:35.
28. Malachi 3:10.
29. Matthew 28:19,20.
30. Matthew 22:36,37.
31. James 2:8; 1:25.
32. 1 Thessalonians 1:3; 2 Thessalonians 1:11.
33. Psalm 32:8.
34. Proverbs 3:5,6.
35. Isaiah 58:11.
36. James 1:5,6.
37. Hebrews 12:1.
38. 1 Corinthians 8:9.
39. 1 Corinthians 10:31.
40. 1 Corinthians 6:19,20.
41. 1 Corinthians 12:13.
42. Colossians 2:10.
43. Colossians 1:18.
44. John 16:14.
45. 1 Peter 3:15.
46. Matthew 10:32.
47. Mark 16:15.

48. See Luke 5:1–11.
49. 1 Peter 5:7.
50. Isaiah 41:10.
51. 1 Samuel 2:30.
52. 2 Corinthians 1:20.
53. Romans 8:35–39.